"Eagles in the

Is a full throttle naughty narrative of what

hang gliding was like in its' "Golden Era".

The ecstasy and agony of the sport where you be-

come a bird at will is poignantly and passionately

depicted in the stories that should be made into a

movie like Dog Town or The Endless Summer.

Great adventure reading.

<u>Rusty Whitley</u>

40 year pilot

Advanced instructor

Honors English student.

EAGLES IN THE FLESH
is
based on a true story.

ERIK B. KAYE

Except for the dead,
all names have been changed
to protect everyone.

EAGLES IN THE FLESH

Author; Erik B. Kaye
LIBRARY OF CONGRESS
COPYRIGHT © TXU 1-802-332
Publisher; Erik B. Kaye
2012 ALL RIGHTS RESERVED

Thankfully Edited By Laura Schiff
LauraSchiff.com

Front Cover Photo;
By Betsy Kendall Bunce
The author launching
from Crested Butte, Colorado.
Photo PG 157 ©Mitch McAleer
Photo PG 166 ©Steve Rodrigues

This Book Is Dedicated To;
Sara Jane Brenner
Allison Kaye Johnson
James A. Zeiset

CONTENTS

CHAPTER ONE

Riders on the storm

Help! Here I am and I think I am going to die! This is what is going through my mind as my teammate CG and I are being yanked backwards through the atmosphere. All I can do is pray; pray that what I see happening to him isn't going to happen to me. Both of us viewing the earth below, both of us know its sight is now a luxury – a luxury that is not going to last. We've left ourselves no way out, no way to escape. It's time to live or die.

Three hundred feet above us is an enormous storm cloud, its dark spinning bottom looking like an upside down whirlpool, its center hole trying to suck us in. Thousands of feet below us, the precious earth looks like a wrinkled piece of soft green felt.

Diving our hang gliders, noses pointed straight down, wings bucking violently, racing futilely for the ground, my mind blaming my teammate for all the things gone wrong; my hands grip the control bar tightly, like a trapeze artist without a net, while I will the glider to go faster, praying for it not to break.

Inside my helmeted head, rushed panic, sweat, and terror.

The wrong cloud, the wrong place, the wrong time, me and CG flying our hang gliders beyond the manufacturer's stated speed limit not to exceed. The gliders push 70 miles per hour as we travel backwards, on the verge of getting sucked uncontrollably up into a huge, black-and-white, lightning-included, cumulonimbus storm cloud.

Like Icarus in the ancient Greek legend , we have flown too close to danger, we have pushed each other too far. Our egos are out of control, dragging us under the bottom of the massive sucking whirlpool.

There are plenty of reasons why we got here, because I am the young upstart pilot and was trying to outperform the older, more experienced CG. That old man has taught me well over the last few years. Too well. It's made me cocky and overconfident, and now it's the student competing against the teacher. No, scratch that - it's student plus teacher competing against Mother Nature, her new rules of survival constantly changing. She shows us no mercy as she drags us higher through the atmosphere.

Today's subject: how to fly a hang glider fast enough to escape the overpowering currents that are getting vacuumed up into the bottom of the wrong cloud. We are trapped under the cloud, like two rats scrambling on a slippery tile floor, trying to escape from being sucked up into an industrial vacuum cleaner, the nozzle of the vacuum, the center of the whirlpool, dragging us into the huge cloud.

With our gliders pointed towards the earth, trying to go down, flying forward as fast as their aerodynamic design will allow, we are still getting sucked up backwards, our progress incorrect. We enter the bottom of the angry cloud, tail first.

Upon entering the storm, all my eyesight goes white. Many shades of white, bright white, gray white, dirty white. A big room filled with white terror, oh yeah, and panic. I can feel the sweat leaking from my helmet, rolling down my forehead, blowing into my eyes, but its salty blindness doesn't matter because on both sides of my eyelids I can see nothing. Strong winds force tears from my eyes, causing my sunglasses to ice over. Thunder cracks inside the storm cloud, shaking my brains. Frustration, fear, anger, terror, panic; powerful emotions churn like an electrical current between my ears.

If I want to live, I think, I got to relax, I got to focus. Focus on what? Everything inside this cloud is a white soaking hell. Relax how? The violent turbulence inside the cloud is thwarting my efforts at keeping the glider from flipping over and breaking. My mind begins losing to panic. I begin feeling small, scared, insignificant, lost in this vast, turbulent, wet, cold, white room. Feeling like a rat in a spinning clothes dryer half full of wet snow. My eyelids start icing up, all ten fingers freezing, my mouth gulping against air sickness.

Oh, God, I pray, get me out of here alive and I will never fly again…

My arms start to tire, my instruments are covered in frost, the wing is handling lethargically, acting like it is covered in ice; I'm losing track of reality, loosing track of time, how long have I been in here, I can't see, help me CG, I want my mom.

I think, I am going to shit my pants and die, and yet I am strangely concerned with the rescue crew finding me with a poop in my pants, and just as I'm contemplating my mortifying end, I see a patch of blue over there at the clouds' border. I dive for the blue, but it keeps moving away, torturing me like a moving target, a target found in an amusement park booth, where the gun is manipulated and one hundred dollars is wasted to get a three dollar teddy bear, I finally hit the elusive target, my reward, punching out the side of the tall white cloud, into the bright blue, blinding sky.

Oh, what a feeling, I am free from that monster, thank God. But just when I think I am saved, I am not, oh no. Disoriented and alone, the earth thousands of feet below me, the features of her surface not making sense, where the hell am I? Cool water droplets run down my face, the ice melting away, the numbers on the defrosted altimeter displaying an astonishing 17,500 feet, my fingers start thawing, my mind enjoys the pain, the pain of life; but that tall evil cloud, the one with the white room, the one that tried to kill me, the one I have just flown out the side of, the one that climbs straight up to 35,000 feet, the one now 3,000 feet below me, the one I was running away from as fast as my wing could fly, the one that made me feel like an insect running from a toppling sky scraper, that one terrifying cloud, it's right over there.

Holy shit, a total rush of hope, one of those flashes you remember for the rest of your life. About 200 feet below me, and a half a mile distant, racing towards the light, I spot my teacher, my best friend, CG. With my head clearing, sun glasses drying, pants clean, I am starting to recognize the features on the earth again. We are deep over the West Elk Wilderness, a landscape of huge, timber-covered mountains without roads, and no places to land. Seeing CG flying off into the distance, heading for the highway and a better life, I am on his tail.

We escape from the storm, figure out where we are, and head south out of the West Elk Mountains. Our next danger, like we need more danger, flying over Black Canyon, a 2,000-foot-deep black gorge cut into the dark rock by a white raging river, and living along its rim an unfriendly tall green forest. We have endured the violence, the blindness, the ice, the turbulence and the white room. All that is left in our path for survival is crossing the Black Canyon.

Then I hear it, a sound that makes me ill, a sound that no hang glider pilot will ever mistake, like two metal baseball bats hitting each other head-on at full swing, the sharp sound of crack-snapping aluminum.

Modern day hang gliders are made out of carbon fiber, heavy duty Dacron, space age Mylar sailcloth, steel cables, and aircraft-grade aluminum. The olden days of bamboo and plastic are long gone, replaced by wings built sleek, fast, stable and strong. Manu-facturers of this type of aircraft put their reputations and lives on the line to perfect the wings they build, and, if I may be so bold as to say it, a hang glider wing is a marvel of modern aviation. These wings we fly are created on drawing boards by designers, perfected on computers by engineers, tested on the backs of trucks, in wind tunnels, and taken to the air by top gun test pilots and amateur adventures like me and CG and our insane crew of fellow pilots affectionately known as Gangreen. For ten years this team of green-clad pilots tested every way possible to break hang gliders, automobiles, hearts, rules and our minds.

In this particular case, the structural glider test being performed by CG is a full dive reaching seventy miles per hour, under a thunder head, attempting to escape the tractor beam suction created by a building storm cloud, while being bounced around by ruthless turbulence, like a golf ball in a cement mixer. This is definitely not in the manual.

We cross the last of the mountain range and are closing in on the rim of the Black Canyon, the least perfect time for his glider to break, when it breaks and goes boom. It is ugly, ugly, ugly; his glider snaps in half, both wings slapping together, pinning CG in the middle, bonding him in the center of the wreckage, like a walnut in the center of a peanut butter and jelly sandwich, his body encased inside the white Wonder Bread. CG, in Gravity's control, is tossed sideways and begins spinning, as if a plane in a World War II movie, with one wing lost, and goes into its spinning death spiral. After three revolutions, the disaster succumbs to gravity and rotates vertically, tumbling unevenly, a flat tire gyrating through the sky. Aluminum tubing tears through the sail, the white and green cloth flaps like a sheet in the wind, the sail cloth contoured around his body, looking like lovers wrapped up in white sheets. I watch as he and his lover, entwined as one, tumble over and over, falling towards the earth.

It is the most helpless I have ever felt, watching as this once-beautiful glider, its wreckage imprisoning CG, falls through the sky, taking my friend away. I watch CG struggling for his life, his limbs continuing to fight the pile of wreckage, the ruins dropping farther away, spiraling down towards the earth, a sumo wrestler wedged in a coffin, tumbling out of an airplane, his fight for escape.

Unprepared to give in and die, struggling against the heavy G-forces hindering his survival, CG battles the flapping, falling wreckage and continues to reach for the handle of his emergency parachute, but gravity is winning and he and his glider continue tumbling end over end. CG is falling to his doom, the earth coming up fast, too fast, his luck running out, good-bye, CG.

From the center of the destruction, out past the wreckage, into the blue sky, a package of life flies; CG's emergency parachute comes alive, like a jellyfish floating in the sky, its canopy opening beautifully, slowing his decent and, of course, it is green, because CG gets a hard-on over anything green.

Thank God, you say, the poor man's troubles are now over, but, oh no, CG's troubles are just about to begin. CG is dropping towards the ground, strapped to a broken, tumbling hang glider, under a storm cloud that wants to kill him, riding an emergency parachute 4,000 feet above the earth, centered over a 2,000-foot-deep Black Canyon. Having no other choice but to negotiate my own troubles, I fly beyond the canyon and lose sight of CG. I've had enough fun for one day, deciding at this point that I cannot outdo CG's present performance, and I begin searching for a safe place to land, vowing to help out later by identifying his body once they drag it out of the canyon.

CG and I were racing in a hang gliding competition when the storm hit, and we had just flown 30 miles from where we launched, attempting to reach the goal field filled with people who are expecting us to land. People and pilots at goal look intently into the sky above the Black Canyon now, searching for the descending CG, all the while listening closely to the communication radios that we carry, as CG gives us the verbal blow-by-blow of his ordeal. The whole crew listens to CG's communications while he descends 4,000 feet, down through the atmosphere at 1,000 feet per minute, the whole calamity headed for the river in the bottom of the Black Canyon in three minutes of ticking time, traveling towards his fate.

(Black Canyon)

"This is CG. I am under emergency parachute deployment about six miles northeast of Cimarron... Oh, shit, I am drifting down into the Black Canyon... Oh, shit, I am going down into the Black Canyon... I am, No- No- No... I am being blown to the north side of the canyon rim... Oh, shit, now I am going in on the south rim... Fuck, I am going into the canyon. No. No. I am going in on the North rim. Yes, the north rim. No, fuck, back to the middle of the canyon. Wait... it is the south side fields. No, it's back to the center of the canyon."

And then, in his panic, a short silence while CG descends to his doom, catching his breath while trying to figure out where he is going to die.

This silence on the radio gives JT – a truly twisted lone eagle of a man, a regular companion of Gangreen – the perfect opportunity to come on the radio and voice his opinion about the childish squealing that CG is making over the airwaves. As CG is 1,000 feet over the Black Canyon and his impending doom, JT says over the radio to CG and for all others to hear:

"CG, just shut up and die like a man."

This comment immediately ratchets CG's voice up a couple of octaves as he announces, with bravado in his tone, to anyone who cares to listen, that he will be crashing into a grove of scrub oak trees 300 feet from the south rim of a 2,000-foot-deep chasm in the black earth. That is it, his final transmission.

I call on the radio for him, "CG, do you copy? CG, do you copy?" His response is silence, nothing, nada, all radio communications lost. The absence of his voice lasts continually, the most deafening silence I have ever felt.

After a long minute, the radio waves crackle back to life and a rescue party is quickly organized, and then dispatched, their destination the south rim of the Black Canyon, the last known direction of CG. An opera of words tumbles forth from the radio as we all converse and wonder about the fate of one we all have lived and loved and flown with. CG, is he dead? Is he dead?

CG is an amazing man, with an engineer's mind and an open and giving heart. He has the ability to be a world class hang glider pilot, but he loves to party; and although he has the ability to be a world class partier, still he loves to hang glide. He is a self-made man that owns a million dollar company and raised two boys on his own. Like me, he can be brilliant one time and a total idiot another. He is a little heavy-set, making the gliders take on more structural stress. He has a huge ego and is Mister Know-It-All, but he never shirked a responsibility and he has been there for more people in need, in the world of hang gliding, than anyone I know.

Ten minutes later, out of the crazy uproar of radio chatter, we hear a small distant voice say, "Hey, shut up, this is CG. I am OK. This is CG. I am OK."

All the radio chatter stops as CG proceeds to give us the location where he's pounded in. You can feel the relief and hear the happy screams of the thirty pilots and support crew as the radio goes berserk. Many a pilot offers to come to his rescue, and plenty show up in the staging area. It takes quite a while for the rescue crew to get up into the forests that surround the Black Canyon and locate him. Thank God for radios, he is found a little shaken and a little scratched up, having descended through some ten-foot-tall scrub oak trees. After giving CG a big hug, the crew proceeds to cut bushes and tree limbs, working hard to disentangle the parachute and broken glider from the forest before dark. Finally the rescue team drives him back to the town of Gunnison, Colorado, where we started this adventure. He walks into the local restaurant, with ten tables full of pilots and friends, and someone stuffs a medicinal double rum and Coke into his hand. Then all hell breaks

loose as he is surrounded by people who love him; hugs and handshakes, laughter and joy, people glad to just look him in the eye
again, happy to see him alive. I remember, as he stood there
among his fans, a crazed new look in his eyes, and a huge smile on
his puss, it was like he saw God. Then, after ten minutes of hugging and hand shaking, the crowd finally settles down and, with
one final chug of his drink, with everyone seated and silent, he
stands and starts to speak. A humbled crowd watches in awe while
this legend of a man, with tears working from his eyes, speaks of
his love for his friends, this world, and his life.

CHAPTER TWO

The Legend of Mount Princeton

CG and I met for the first time at the end of a dangerous, bumpy, 4x4 road, below the peak of Mount Princeton in Colorado. The steep, twisting granite road, a torturous two-wheel track that threads its way through gnarly ancient forests, splashes over a couple of broken truck creek crossings, past a muffler-crunching big boulder scramble, and then sneaks past cliffs and voids to break out above the timberline, comes to a halt in thin air at 12,200 feet above sea level.   Here the road builders employed their skills with explosives, slicing open the mountain's face, the tall broken granite boulders lining the sides of the slice, looking like rows of stone houses in a field. Here is where one must change vehicles from truck to glider in order to proceed any farther.

CG was standing at the end of the road, beside his dark green, one-ton, Ford monster van: the mass of steel and rubber looking too top heavy, as if one sharp corner and the wheels would be facing up. The van's body stood on extra tall, extra wide, deeply treaded, reptile traction off-road tires, the door height causing the passengers to ascend to enter. Bolted to the roof of the machinery, a glider rack, fashioned from one quarter inch polished steel that flashed in the sun, creating, as an end product, a sparkling king's crown. The Mountain King, as the van is affectionately named, was always overloaded with gear, gliders and pilots.

As I learned in the coming years, CG drove the Mountain King as if driving a race car with his balls on fire; the tires spitting gravel, its mass barreling full blast up the granite mountain, velocity everywhere all the time. Give me full warp drive, Mr. Scott, damn the suspension, we got to go flying. An experience in the King goes something like this: the gas pedal or brake pedal are interchangeably mashed to the floor; the large V10 engine, either full on or full off, the exhaust pipe screaming deep yodels against the mountain side, loose objects in the cubicle sliding back and forth in rhythm with the pedals as the bouncing scenery whizzes by, along with the increased heartbeats of the van's occupants. This speeding chunk of metal threads through trees, boulders, sheer cliffs, and other vehicles as CG attempts to push the limits of the van, its passengers swaying in rhythm with the road, their white knuckled hands reaching for a hold, grasping to stay in place and avoid knocking heads with their neighbors. Finally, a victim's psychological boundaries are breached, a shaken soul cries out in fear, "CG, please slow the fuck down." This, of course, makes CG go faster, escalating the victim's dread, each individual in the bouncing cage an undergraduate of CG's master class on insanity.

Pilots and passengers from around the world smile in fear when recalling their experiences in the Mountain King. After one particularly electrifying ride up the snow-covered Mount Princeton road, my sister turned to me and said, her voice oddly more strained than usual, "I. Will. Never-never-ever-ever get in that… Thing…again." I always trusted CG.

With his reputation as a big, bad, famous sky god, my first impression of CG is that he looks like a big, soft teddy bear, but on closer inspection, his eyes beam controlled insanity – a possible breeding between Smokey the Bear and Evel Knievel.

CG is a selfless lover of anything involving hang gliding. His attitude is you are welcome to come along for the ride, I will help you all I can, try to keep up, and don't get killed.

In the hang gliding world, CG, Gangreen and the Mountain King are legendary, as are CG's driving skills, insanity and dogged determination. In his capable hands, the van bounces and slides to locations beyond the end of the road, beyond the demands of Gangreen, places without roads, where passengers call forward progress impossible; horrible places, where the van slants so steeply on hillsides that even I want to get out and walk; places so far beyond the road, so deep into No Man's Land, that if the bouncing van broke down, no hungry, small-town, damn-the-money tow truck driver would ever come to save us. We find ourselves in this dangerous position many times over the years: inching forward, forcing ourselves to continue, to save the life of a missing pilot, a brother or sister in danger – cold, wet, injured, lost, the victim having no realistic hope of rescue except by fellow pilots in the Mountain King. Rescuers who are pilots, and who think like pilots, who are able to track a flight path starting from the vanished pilot's last known point of communication, follow a logical train of thought, reading the winds, the terrain, the storms; they have the right maps, use the right technology: robust radios, high-powered binoculars, bolt cutters for fences and locks, high clearance tires for deep sage, deep water, deep shit; driving to elevated points in search of the lost, giving the rescued soul medical attention when necessary, and a rum and Coke when needed.

My first time flying with the legend of Mount Princeton, I park in the lower lot and hike up the last stretch of road, hoping to meet with the group of pilots spilling out of the Mountain King. I notice CG immediately, his body language excited, like that of a young child's; the body language of his passengers, like those of humans recovering from distress. Obviously, they'd never ridden with CG before and had to see it to disbelieve. CG, as usual, is giving a long-winded explanation. CG is always giving long-winded explanations. This one is about his special technique for dislodging the unwieldy, 16-foot-long, 60-pound hang gliders from the top of the van, eight feet in the air, down to the ground without any damage to person, place or thing.

As I pitch in and help to unload the gliders, one of the pilots in the mix introduces me to CG. We shake hands, look each other in the eye and think hello. Little do I realize at the time that our pressing of palms is the start of Gangreen, a fifteen year adventure that truly flew into the wild blue yonder, an adventure that constructed my life, tried to end it, and, ultimately, one that will never be repeated again, except in this book.

At the end of the road, on top of one of the world's most demanding hang gliding sites, I ask CG if he can be my teacher, give me some education on how to fly Mount Princeton. He opens his mouth and, after his 30-minute dissertation, I am overloaded with more information that any human can possibly comprehend. It's like opening a fire hydrant full of knowledge. The lecture includes geology, meteorology, over-the-top aerodynamics combined with Einstein's theory of relativity, and, of course, three stories about himself. The launch is dangerous, he says; it stands on a knife's edge ridge, meaning that when the powerful thermals come racing up both sides of the mountain, they simultaneously breed with each other on launch, creating powerful dust devils, freaks of nature that have been known to pick up the unlucky pilot and glider, tossing them without mercy into the boulder field like a wet dish rag, so don't wait on launch too long. Also, his lecture continues, launching at 12,200 feet above sea level, where the air is thinner, is like the difference between milk and a milk shake, so the hang glider is not going to just fly off of launch nice and creamy, so run hard. If you survive the launch and are not climbing over the main ridge, follow the long jagged spine over the chalk-colored cliffs (where another pilot got killed), and head for the LZ (landing zone), looking for lift all the way. When you come into the landing area, where three large canyons come together, the winds will change direction, so be able to change with them or crash.

I was a relatively new pilot at that time, with not a lot of air time under my belt. My hang gliding experience included a few short exciting hops, a couple of high flights calculated in minutes, a couple dozen launches and landings, a few good crashes, and a burning desire to fly like the eagles. My arsenal included a third-hand used glider, with a couple pieces of dirty, sun-burnt duct tape holding it together. My head was protected by a well-scratched black helmet. In my bag was some other beat-up, though function-al, equipment, including a pair of old leather hiking boots, the bot-toms, once proud, now worn down to equal the traction of Formi-ca. I drove an abused Volkswagen square-back with one side bashed in, the vehicle smoking oil so badly that, from 300 feet up, the wind direction could be observed for landing. Check the gas and fill the oil. Thus was the extent of my equipment.

Ignorance is my strong suit, and I learn the hard way that CG's idea of being my teacher is to throw me into the sky and see what happens. You know the old sink or swim scale. This type of education is a great way to gain needed flying skills quickly, but your survivability rate is squat.

My launch from Mount Princeton goes well, and I give my-self a B+ for effort, but the huge gray chalk cliffs, which resemble dentist drilling anxiety, scare the living shit out of me, so I fuck up and fly out over the valley, just like I was told not to, and there I fail to climb in broken lift. After making multiple mistakes, I find myself far back in the canyon, leaving myself no hope of gliding to the LZ.

My understanding of my mistakes should at least give me the grade of C, maybe. Underneath me, a canyon carpeted in 80-foot-tall Ponderosa pine trees and mountains of solid granite that fence me in, make my only hope of landing softly look like a pimple on the face of Godzilla: a very, very small sagebrush-covered spot bordered by tall, solid brown trees whose fluctuating branches are just waiting to snag me and yank me out of the sky, possibly placing my blood on the wrong side of my skin.

I have an ego and I blame it for putting me in this predicament as I circle over the spot. I blame it for my solid lack of good judgment and I blame it for trying to kill us and, hopefully, when I finally do come to a stop, on the spot, hopefully only my ego is going to get hurt.

Circling 300 feet over trees, I study up for my first final exam as CG's apprentice: how to survive in the face of sure disaster. I am hoping to pass this lesson with a grade of D, because an F grade is going to get me expelled from the planet. Committed, flying in circles lower and lower over the small field, my terror increasing exponentially with every foot I sink down, adrenalin chasing through my veins, my helmet beginning to sweat, I position my glider for the landing approach, my decisions in question, asking myself if this is going to be a very short and painful hang gliding career. I've been hearing all my life, terror brings out people's strengths, and at 150 feet over the spot I am strong as an elephant on Viagra. Oh, shit, here I go. Seeing the branches of tall pine trees thrashing around in the strong winds, I pull on more speed while I panic harder, as my glider rocks in the windy turbulence like a sailboat in a storm.

I bank the big bird up onto a wing tip, carving onto final approach, and fight my bouncing glider out of the turn and onto a straight and level flight, only inches over the tops of the trees. I cross the last of the tree tops, diving my wing down into the meadow without catching any glider parts on the uneven tree tops, and pass my first examination, giving myself another B+. I begin the next test by arriving way too fast in an opening among the trees, the slippery glider hauling ass, leveling out ten feet above the ground, my math skills calculating in the negative the amount of room necessary to slow down, my large diameter eyes watching the trees at the other end of the field approaching to eat me.

Do you know that bad feeling when your foot has stomped the brakes down to the floor and nothing happens, and your car keeps sliding on the icy road and still nothing happens, and your heart moves into your throat and, again, nothing happens, and you keep stomping as your car just keeps sliding out of control, your bumper soon to make contact with the lettering on the car, stopped at the light in front of you, that reads State Patrol? I am having that stomping on the brakes feeling, realizing there will be no stopping before entering the inflexible forest on the other end of the field. Aiming my body for the biggest opening between the hard brown tree trunks, I rock myself upright, grab the vertical down tubes, reposition my head from its place as my front bumper, drop my legs out of the harness and drag them through the sage brush hoping this maneuver will slow me down, quickly realizing what a painful idea that is. Not slowing this glider down means more pain is coming. I take a chance and quickly push the glider's nose up, the reaction lifting me twenty feet into the air; just enough to slow the beast down ten miles per hour, and just as quickly I pull the control bar back, speeding it up to keep from stalling. This action, I imagine, eliminating ten more weaves from my future line of stitches. I give myself a grade of C for that one.

As the glider continues advancing and leveling out ten feet above the ground, my fragile body enters the forest, traveling Emergency Room fast. It is then that I pull the magic rabbit out of

my ass. I shove the nose of the glider straight up, hoping my fool-
ish panicked action will bring me to a complete stop. Only a violent and insane reaction is going to stop my forward thrust, but
now what? As Einstein once said, with all action there is an equal
and opposite reaction. My forward momentum transforms into
vertical momentum as I ascend hastily against gravity, climbing 30
feet into the air, and then smashing, like a crash test dummy, into
the overhead outspread branches and soft clingy pine needles,
coming to a complete stall.

At this point, the glider's dive recovery system should have
kicked in, causing me to lose all control of the glider. It's designed
to recover from a stall by rotating the nose over, pointing it straight
down at the ground, and picking up speed, thereby catching up
with gravity. Then, with me at the glider's mercy, the son of a
bitch would pile drive me like a jackhammer, right into the earth.
To this day I am not sure who won the coin toss, pure luck or my
guardian angel, but my momentum buries the glider deeply into the
interlaced branches, which snag the upper rigging of the glider,
like an aircraft carrier arresting cable snagging a speeding jet, the
trees hold on to my dive recovery wires and cause the merciless
object strapped to my back to come to a complete stop a good 200
stitches above the forest floor.

I think, "Great, a pile drive impact from 20 feet is better than
all the above. Hell, even if I get carried out of this field on a
stretcher, I may get a B for this action." Pine needles rain down
upon my life, the branches and glider slam dancing violently together, the impact pulling the glider's controls out of my hands,
rattling me around inside the control frame tubing. There I hang,
supported by the tree limbs like a scarecrow in a noose, and when
the judgment hammer drops, the weight of us - me, my glider, and
my guardian angel – all three of us are slowly lowered by gravity,

back down to the ground. I hit the dirt ass first, the glider fol[l]ing me from the large pine tree, like a lead Christmas ornament, base tube resting in my lap. I sit there stunned, the branches above swaying "you're welcome," my mind waiting for some kind of pain to hit. A few seconds of eternity pass before I realize I am pain free.

I live through CG's first class, hoping he will at least give me an A for effort. I radio to him that I am good and will be able to walk to the road under my own power. He replies, "I thought we were going to have to ruin a perfectly good flight to scrape you off those trees." Oh, to live and fly another day! Isn't life great! I know then that I've passed my first class with the master.

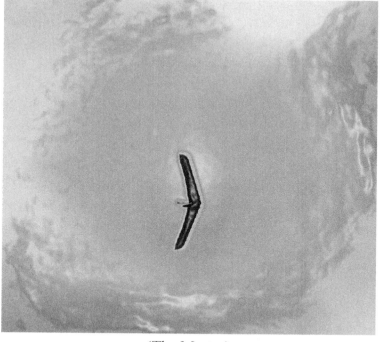

(The Master)

CHAPTER THREE

Stairway to Heaven

sky, eye to eye with the eagles, my body
... by wings, its weight liberated from gravity, wings lifted by
the winds, blowing me to places previously unreachable, previously unexplored, with no fences, no boundaries, learning the sky,
my playground the soft white clouds. This is what I have dreamed
of, to soar like a bird, flying circles overhead, to ride the invisible
currents.

What are your dreams of flying? Perhaps, like Aladdin, you
float cross-legged on a magic carpet, smoking a hookah, hovering
in and out of clouds, gazing lazily down on a white sandy beach
full of naked sunbathers. Or possibly you prefer airborne propulsion like Mary Poppins, with her high-performance magic umbrella. You lift vertically off the ground, soaring at amazing speeds
past the neighbors, always in style, your clothing never ruffled,
your hair unaffected by the winds. You land softly on your feet
and close your turbo-charged sun shade, your commute to work
completed. Maybe you prefer to fly at night, past the glow of the
moon, cackling on a witch's broom. Or like Superman, in a waving cape over tight aerodynamic clothing. Arms outstretched, fingers slicing the air, you fly through the stratosphere as you race to
save the earth, landing in time to rescue a damsel in distress. You
lift her into your arms and transport her high up to a mountain
condo for a little romantic interlude. Yeah, I like that one.

For my money, the most exciting way to soar in the sky like
the birds is by hang gliding, which entails circling up in the warm
currents of air called thermals. If you could see these thermals that
the eagles, hawks and hang gliders use to rise up into the sky, they
would look like miniature tornados, like the tornados you see on

TV, except friendlier. A tornado compared to a thermal is like a car wreck compared to a sail boat ride. A tornado is just an extra strong thermal that just happens to lift cars and houses, spitting out trees and lives.

Birds, bugs, plastic bags, straw, and hang gliders ride into the sky on these invisible, elusive, multi-dimensional columns of lifting air. Riding these thermals takes practice. Gaining a feel for how they work is essential if you wish to survive. To navigate thermals, hang glider pilots use a special singing instrument called a Vario, its computer voice trilling a slow ballad when the thermal's rate of climb is mellow; when the rate of climb is forceful, the Vario belts out "Rock Around the Thermal," in its beeping, bopping Vario way, and when the Vario gets a-rockin', hang on, because this is where life gets exciting. Imagine riding an aggressive rollercoaster while lying on a spinning merry-go-round.

Thermal power changes as the day's heating progresses. The morning starts off calmly, the sun starts to rise, its rays deflect off the ground, the earth's crust slowly heats, and thermals are put into motion. You can sense them in the wind, a pressure against the skin, a spinning, swirling feel indicates their presence. The first thermals of the day are like a waltz: slow, smooth and flowing evenly, their power increases as the sun follows it arc, the ground gets hotter, increasing the wind. The thermal waltz becomes a salsa, with quicker energy and more feisty passion; the sun advances and the winds blast out rock and roll, then hang on, baby, hang on as Mother Nature pushes the dance vertically and you and your hang glider are thrown into the mosh pit at the sun's zenith of power. Then, as the sun sinks towards the west, the ecstatic dance slowly returns to the lilting waltz and darkness. Mother Nature damn near does the same old thing every day, all over the world, dancing from the flatlands of Kansas to the rice patties of Thailand.

Thermals are shape-shifters, and it's always a challenge to fly inside one of them as they take the form of a tornado funnel, a column, a mushroom, a snake twisting around you. Pushed and stirred by the wind, thermals often have elusive personalities; you could say they're like people: some you like, and some... well, some have an attitude. Like a bull trying to remove the human on its back, a swirling, bucking thermal is always trying to spit you out, always testing the pilot's aptitude, experience and luck.

How you fly a hang glider in these thermals is like this: picture yourself riding a bicycle, breathlessly, as it lifts off the ground – just like ET in the basket of Elliot's bike. The sensation of the thermal lifting you up is extremely exciting. Time to concentrate now: if you keep going straight, you will ride out the other side of the thermal. Quickly regain your composure and circle back into the lift. Quality coordinated thermal flying means staying inside the lift, making the right sized turns, controlling your speed; to go faster, pull the control bar in, to go slower, push it out. Swing your weight to the left move left, and now sway it to the right. Dance with Mother Nature inside that column of air, letting her lift you into the developing cloud above. When the thermals are big and fat, she is easier to follow, and you can go slower with lots of room to play. When the thermals are small and strong, they require more skill, faster speed, higher bank angles, and tighter circles. Don't get cocky or push her too hard, or she can kill you without mercy. But once you have circled the skies with Mother Nature as your dance partner, you will look at clouds with the eyes of a bird, you will taste cotton candy skies that are finer than wine, finer even than Acapulco gold, the taste of fleeting clouds.

A pilot's reward for deciphering the thermal's mystery is to gain contact with the base of a cloud. According to Nature's law, upon reaching the top of a thermal, the lifting air diminishes and stops, replaced with moist air that forms a cloud. Touching the base of the clouds is a thrill, giving aviators the feeling of having arrived at Heaven's doorstep. It is an unparalleled experience for any human. That's Nature's law. The laws of Man make it illegal to fly inside the clouds with a hang glider, and what patriotic American would want to break those laws?

At cloud base, gravity takes over. The lift is gone and it's time to go fishing for another thermal. A pilot's height over the earth's surface dictates the amount of leeway available to accomplish this goal. If another thermal is found, we spiral up again for another taste of heaven; if not, we either land beautifully on the earth and celebrate with a cold brew, or we whack ungracefully into the ground – blowing our landing, lying in the dirt, eating dust and washing it down with a cold brew.

Inebriated pilots sit at the watering hole and share thermal stories. The more beer, the better the stories, and the more tips the bartender makes. The pilots slur that the thermal was like an elevator ride to the clouds – fat, wide and smooth, with not a bump; or, "It yanked me into the sky like a rocket, so violent that I almost shit my pants." The more powerful the drinks, the bigger the adventure stories told by the hang glider pilots, the bird men who fly to Dreamland.

Since before humans could produce fire, they have dreamed of flying. Constantly probing their minds for a way to duplicate the birds, a way to make life easier, helping to improve travel, give man a better view for finding food and hiding food. Flying would help the primitive man avoid being food, and the pleasure of flight could be amazing. We wanted it, and, like a stubborn child crying for a toy, we were going to get it.

Mankind labored for centuries, experimenting with any objects that could facilitate flying: tree bark, buffalo hides, cotton sheets, plywood cutouts, large palm leaves attached to bamboo cages; amazing, unproven contraptions built by wise men who promised superior flying ships. Gravity inevitably had its way with these early aviators, killing the adventurers and returning their outdated designs to the hard, hard, ground. The stairway to the heavens was agonizingly slow and brutal, as if God held back the best for last. Finally, after many deaths and thousands of broken bones, the world's most famous bicycle builders got it right. The dream became reality. In the record books, the Wright brothers first sustained human flight in Kitty Hawk, NC on December 17, 1903.

But let's not leave out the possibility of the first unrecorded human flight: before the Wright Brothers, before written language, before pencil and paper, there was Argentavis magnificens. Literally, "magnificent Argentine bird," this monster of the avian kingdom is the largest bird ever discovered, weighing in at 170 pounds, with a wingspan of 23 feet, I like to think that Argentavis magnificens could have made for one heck of a wild ride for some adventurous ancestor of homo sapiens.

Picture with me a brave, beautiful, somewhat crazy cavewoman and her desire to fly. By day, she studies the magnificent Argentine bird, with its wingspan more than five times the length of her own body. It soars overhead, black wings blotting out the sun, its screams shaking the ground. She observes the animal's mobility, its patterns, its flying speeds and circle sizes. The gust from its great black wings blows her hair back, causing her body to give an involuntary shudder. She is in awe of the majestic and terrifying beast. By night, she dreams of capturing the fearsome creature and flying on its back to faraway lands, the envy of her entire clan. She awakens, trembling with desire.

Years pass, the cavewoman's dream of flying slipping by. She's in her old age, alone, the kids now grown, the mate gone, life's spark cooled but not dead. Her hunger to fly keeps her going. Her body is worn, but her time has come. She has a plan. As she expected, Argentavis magnificens circles up the mountain face, gaining in altitude, its flight closing in on her position. She prepares herself. The enormous bird flies slowly under the cavewoman's cliff. Her heart screams, her primitive mind calculates, Now: she climbs out of the cave, starting to run, reaching full speed at the edge of the cliff, and leaps off into the void, her arms wide, her hair whipped by the wind, her deer skin coat open as if a small parachute helping to steer her fall, her body shakes in terror, her timing perfect. She lands hard, grabbing hold of the bird's mane, quickly wrapping her legs around the feathered flesh. With another swing of the creature's great wings, the cavewoman's dreams become reality. She flies.

Fortunately, learning to fly is much easier and safer today than when the cavewoman was alive. With the right training, a pair of wings, some good weather, and a little work, someday maybe you will fly, like Argentavis magnificens, beyond the immortal cavewoman's cliff. You can find a hang gliding school at www.USHPA.com. It will be a fun school, a place where the instructors love to teach people, helping to fulfill their dreams. Do it. Do it now, before you are too old, lying in a strange bed, in a place full of strange people, with a tube up your ass and your dreams have passed you by. Most schools will set you up with a pair of wings and supply you with all the equipment you'll need. Then they'll check your physiological profile to ascertain if you are insane.

Before I learned to fly, I was broke, homeless, unemployed and lonely. Just out of college, I spent the summers hiking and winters as a ski bum. Home was a camping tent outside of a mountain mining town. My only ambitions: to get laid and to not get mauled by bears. I was in love with Colorado. Then the bears tore up my tent and I shattered my ankle skiing. Two surgeries later, it seemed my life had taken a U-turn. This was when true friends from my college days came to my rescue and put me up in their home while I recovered. There was a reason for my pain. It was so I could sit on their couch and study every hang gliding magazine they had. Yes, they helped me. As soon as I could walk again, they sent me off to hang gliding school.

My first lesson was on a small hill covered in grass and a few knee-high pointy yucca plants for obstacles. In the distance, a view of tall Rocky Mountains, their caps white with snow, cold high peaks a perfect contrast to the warm winds that lifted the stable glider from my shoulders. The breeze blowing into my face helped cool the hot sweat that dripped out of my helmet, a combination of excitement and fear. Holding the glider correctly, taking a few tentative steps down the hill, moving the wing forward into the wind, feeling the weight of the glider lifting from my shoulders, running faster, more excited, the extra speed lifting the glider higher and me up with it, my heart jumping, its energy pumping faster, my feet leaving the ground, still running, running in the air, like a propeller. My feelings were unlike any other. My body floated in space, generating a new, unexpected experience. It was like an orgasm, but softer, like a carnival ride, but freer; the wind a new friend, the ground something of the past, the sky a new lover. Slowing down, I rotated the glider's nose skyward, exposing its underside to the winds, timing the flair of the wing correctly, my glider settling back to earth. My feet came to a stop, but my heart never did.

Things were looking up. My life as a hang glider junkie included getting fired by a boss fed up with too many sick days taken off to feed my adrenaline addiction, empty bank accounts, girlfriend shouting, "You love that glider more than me," as she walks out the door, the car badly leaking oil, time for a newer one, a bigger one, a better one, big enough to sleep in, because the rent money just flew away in the last thermal. My travels included dragging a heavy hang glider in a twenty-foot-long cardboard box across the floor of an airport terminal full of people, all of them shuffling to get out of the way while giving me the evil eye as I straight line it to the counter of United Airlines. The attendant, having her doubts, watches the mess pull up, knowing that hang gliders are not allowed on commercial airliners. I, in my hang gliding T-shirt, flash her a smile and swear straight to her face that I'm a law abiding citizen. The big red letters on the box beside me read FRAGILE: POLE VAULTING EQUIPMENT.

Truthfully, I was a punk. But Mother Nature schools pilots in many ways. I attended one tough class of hers in the Colorado Rockies in mid-summer. I was flying early in the day, on the sunny side of the mountain range, conditions excellent, thermals, smooth and abundant. I floated around at cloud base, at one with my glider, Mother Nature's views from this altitude, stunning.

She giveth, and then she taketh away.

My lesson started twenty miles away, on the opposite side of the mountain range, as a pocket of moist air heated up, building the moisture into large clouds. Not to worry because I was not paying attention. Very quickly, the clouds that were small are now very tall, bubbling into beautiful but serious thunder heads, their tops reaching 35,000 feet. Finally, I, the punk kid with the iPod, not paying attention at the back of the class, face up to reality and register the dangerous, but distant, storm possibility.

Still, I felt little concern. I was flying plenty far away from the storm, floating around in the most beautiful sky, its deep blue dotted with nice puffy white clouds, climbing in friendly thermals. Life just doesn't get any better than this. Ok, smart ass, lesson #1.

I see lightning and rain coming out of the storm, but believe, foolishly, that I can get back on the ground whenever I want, way before that big nasty cloud, on the other side of the mountain range, turns into a raining- hailing- windy- dusty- gust front storm. A gust front is big fear. For non-motorized flying contraptions, the only hope of escape is to outrun it, but if you end up running out of altitude before you escape, then you are in big trouble, punk. I stayed in the air just a little longer. Bad mistake, yes sir, big bad mistake.

From the exploding thunder storm, falling rains pushed over to the sunny side of the mountain range, creating high winds that pushed dust clouds in my direction. The smart pilots – the ones that paid attention and sat in the front of the class – they are running from the soil-filled wall that is hastily marching across the landscape, catching the fool in the back of the class off guard. This incoming storm squeezes like a wave against the air mass that I am flying in, on what used to be the fun side of the mountain range, every molecule of air trying to get out of the way of the dust-filled wave streaming across the desert towards me, now lifting me up like a space shuttle, giving me an elevator ride to the moon.

I start getting cold. The ride gets more turbulent. The views from 18,000 feet are spectacular when my oxygen tank runs out

and my drinking water freezes. My mind starts to come unglued.
Brain cells dying. Fingers and face numbing.

But I have a plan. I call it Plan A. Fly ahead of the storm,
beyond the lightning, beyond the nasty winds, rain, hail, mud, danger. Get back on the ground, landing safely in one piece, right next
to a bar. Leisurely, I unhook myself from the glider, put it back in
the bag, and accept the margarita being handed by a Senorita. I
climb up on a bar stool, and, with cocktail in hand, watch the passing storm through the barroom window.

Yeah, right.

Suddenly, I am awakened by the teacher, the gust front racing underneath me. Oops, big mistake, numbers two and three.
Mother Nature turns into a raving bitch. The air is lifting so fast,
like a runaway elevator, racing to bust through the roof of a sky
scraper, I can't get down. The beautiful landing area I had picked
out earlier is swirling with dust, looking like a cat fight. Violent
turbulence tosses me wildly, my glider barely controllable. The
thrashing I am receiving is tiring my body. My poor brain matter
is turning into airborne Jell-O.

Eighteen thousand feet, time to escape from the storm. My
control bar is pulled hard into my knees, placing me in the fetal
position, a position that takes a lot of effort, a position that I only
use for run-away speeds. The wind speed meter attached to my
base tube bounces between fifty and sixty mph. From the cloud
above, it starts to rain ice pellets, their clatter bouncing loudly on
my helmet. I am wet, then cold, as I bounce around in the turbulence. I am a snowman, careening down a mogul field, strapped to
a toboggan. I'm thrown backwards, then pulled forward, sunglasses plastered in snot that just got yanked from my nose. I can't see
shit.

Not today for plan A. Today is plan F.

Plan F: The storm has now invaded the area previously known as civilization, forcing me over the horizon into No Man's Land, with few roads, no people, and no bars. After an agonizing ten mile glide, reaching beyond the edge of the storm, running out of altitude, out of water, hypoxic, cold, hungry, tired, battling for survival, finally I glide to a reasonable landing field, landing a half a mile away from a lonely dirt road, in the middle of nowhere, out of radio contact with my chase crew on the ground. I land hard, unhook from the glider, struggle to its front, and grab the nose wires, holding on tightly. No time to take off my harness or helmet, I pray that the glider is not ripped from my hands as the ferocious storm hits me. High winds, dust clouds, rain, hail; a young punk caught by a gust front in the high desert. Dust is driven into my eyes, my mouth, my helmet. Like a leashed cat, my glider bucks as I hang on. Right behind the bad tasting dust comes a downpour of rain, my helmet, sunglasses, glider all streaked with mud. My mouth grinds with dust, red sunburnt lips, picture frame around my brown, dust-coated teeth. I am quite the portrait, a colorful smile installed on my face. God, do I need a beer.

Dogz

CHAPTER FOUR

Dinosaur, CO.

Dinosaur, Colorado, so named for the nearby National Dinosaur Monument, is a splat on the northwest corner of the map, on the Utah border. The town has absorbed a few well-weathered houses, a gas station, a rustic western hotel, one restaurant and, thank God, a liquor store; great locals, a few friendly dogs and a few unfriendly dogs. Many competitive hang glider pilots travel thousands of miles to the high desert of Dinosaur, wanting a taste of its famous air, to test their skills against 120 of the world's best pilots, racing each other through the sky on a new class of competition gliders, testing fancy prototype equipment, swapping stories and glider parts, chasing future lovers and running from exes, playing with old friends, making new ones, the whole group of people a traveling entourage, like a big family on a flying tour, everyone headed to the week-long United States of America National Hang Gliding Championships.

Living in the vegetation close to town are wild animals, animals that are a little smaller than the dinosaurs who roamed here millions of years ago, but no less volatile: coyotes, bears, mountain lions, rattle snakes, armies of Mormon crickets, and monster packrats, all hunting for deer, elk and any stray house pet that wanders too far from town. Past and present Dinosaur is no place for the weak; one dinosaur's arm bone is as big as your leg. To stay alive, the dinosaurs ran fast, watched their backs, hid from danger, hunted every day, and roamed vast amounts of rugged country, where other dinosaurs with sharp teeth lived by tearing each other apart, then swallowing each other in chunks. It was the Law of the Jungle, a world where luck was short and the weak lived to be eaten.

Each day in Dinosaur starts about the same: a beautiful summer Colorado morning, the sky cawing with crows spewing their raspy voices into the bright blue sky, songbirds flittering between the branches of their cedar playground, their voices singing for the invaders of their forest, the rising sun's rays deflecting off the vast expanses of purple-green sage, concentrating its light against the distant mountains that are glowing purple mountain majesty, and preparing themselves for another day of thermal generation.

Pilots arrive from town and park in the green mountain meadow at launch, unload their gliders and begin to metamorphose their long cocoon tubes into bright beautiful butterfly wings, as if the spawning of butterflies brought friendship to the watching wild winged creatures.

The hundreds of lonely miles surrounding Dinosaur are exotic and wild, the country opening down in the lowlands consisting of dry desert, mostly light brown hills, ravines, rocks and boulders strewn about, where the water seldom flows and all the desert plants and animals are ready to bite you, sting you, poison you, or remind you that the last place you carelessly sat down was a mistake, the narrow snaky patches of dark brown and yellow cactus whisper of water flowing there months ago. Rolling quietly up out of the desert are vast green and purple sage brush plateaus dotted with patches of small forests, where tall black and green trees cast the only shadows for miles on the animals hiding beneath them from the hot sun. Squiggly lines, painted with red, brown and green scrub oak, follow the winding flow of the water's calling, the sage brush ending abruptly at the edge of a meandering cliff, eroded in place by a deep cut river canyon. Water the color of peanut butter bounces against the ancient river canyon walls, pocked with caves, the walls painted with multiple colors, as if drawn by a child holding half the Crayola Crayon colors in one hand, and sweeping them along the canyon's canvas. A wild roiling river drains from the many lonely mountains, their distant black peaks dotted with snow, protruding above dark green forest. Feelings of remote, small, lonesome, free, part of nature, a place where we come from, opening the soul, no measurements in the vastness, back in time,

quiet, more peaceful, less movement, self-aware… a place called
Dinosaur. I wish I could explain it better, but you have to see it to
feel it.

The hang gliding site at Dinosaur is ideal; it simply can be
called a thermal manufacturer. This incredible wall of rock faces
south, directly into the eye of the burning high desert sun. At
dawn each day the rays of the sun appear over the eastern horizon,
slowly heating the desert floor as if heating an aluminum pan on a
gas stove, thermals slowly bubbling up from the bottom, up along
the dark rocky ridge, bringing the crows, hawks and eagles up inside them. And the higher the sun gets, the hotter the desert floor
gets, until, finally, the boiling, lifting energy racing up the mountain face creates a sound like that of a jet, the trees dancing in the
wind giving a hiss as the energy fights to get through the pine
boughs, the commanding presence of the powerful thermals working on the psyches of the hang glider pilots, who, in the shade of
the trees, are preparing their equipment and soon will be throwing
themselves off into the noisy abyss.

Tall, fat, powerful, ominous clouds build early in the day,
climbing up over the distant Uinta mountain range, which usually
means storms and gust fronts, a good possibility of high winds and
pain. Pilots socialize at the launch site, 60 miles away, in the vast,
shadowed country below, telling their cloud stories and watching
for the possibility of big storms and danger; you could feel the fear
in the air.

The task for today is designed to be short, meaning we will
be in the air less time than usual, consequently avoiding the dangerous storms that surely will be blowing our way. The cliff edge
that we fly from is a 2,000-feet-tall, ten-miles-long thrust, straight
up out of the desert, a jagged black-and-white mountain base
striped with purple, brown and gray cliffs, cruel cliffs, barbed and

looming, which create an imposing barrier, almost as if the cliffs are defending the face of the mountain. A few old, twisted, green and gray trees perch, like gargoyles, on the edges of the cliffs, tall brown and green pine forests closely rim the top of the flat mountain, the border of trees looking like guards marching in file along a fortress rampart, inspecting the desert below, the whole scene coming across like a dragon castle.

"Dino" Launch

Soaring at Dinosaur is very dynamic. In the early morning and late afternoon, light ridge lift and soft thermals deflect upwards along the mountain's face, creating a relaxed and low-stress flying experience. Ridge lift is created when wind blowing against a hill climbs up above the top, giving a magic cushion of invisible atmosphere to be floated on above the ridge. Ridge lift is easy. It creates a large lifting thoroughfare, like a vertical wind tunnel, a cushion of air that is a highway for flying back and forth, a place in which to just float around, relax, enjoy the view, practice your skills, a place where pilots can mingle, a place to wait for the next thermal. But in the summer, during the middle of the day, the flying conditions are like traveling through a pot of boiling water. Rates of climb inside thermals, as well as rates of sink next to the thermals, are in the 1,000- to 2,000-foot-per-minute range. It's like climbing to the top of a large skyscraper one minute, and falling to the sidewalk the next. Pilots circling in a wild exchange of lifting and sinking experience G forces, like being on the outside of a crack-the-whip ride, while standing in the center of a spinning merry-go-round, with a ten pound barbell in each hand, the weights trying to pull you to the outside of the turns while you fight to stay inside the turn – your arms working overtime, the physical art of keeping the nose of the glider from getting yanked straight up and stalling, or straight down and losing altitude. Then comes the psychological struggle; the mental transition from spinning up at 1,500-feet-per-minute, gaining 8,000 feet, to dropping down to 1,500-feet-a-minute while traveling miles through the atmosphere across the earth is dazzling, it's an experience that astonishes the mind, creates a rush of adrenalin and freedom and floating, steering a smorgasbord of emotions to exercise the heart. Why do we fly at Dinosaur? Because (no, I am not kidding you) we can fly cross-country for hours, covering over a hundred miles in a single flight, many pilots gaining altitudes of 15,000 feet, with a handful of sky gods touching heaven at 20,000 feet, birdmen climbing in and gliding between 10 to 15 thermals and completing an amazingly long flight.

Back on the ground, five respected pilots are voted in as the task committee. The task committee's job is to decipher the weather reports, then debate and agree on where and how far the pilots will be flying to reach our goal on any given day. Once the task committee, along with the meet director, comes up with the task for the day, they then write their decision on a chalkboard set up next to launch. The board includes pictures, diagrams and weather data posted in graphs and numbers, and is understood by all except us dopers. Over the years, I quit trying to figure out the mathematical weather gibberish. My attitude being, "The sun is up, let's go fly." Within five minutes of the task board being posted, and the distant clouds getting bigger, pilots start whining to the red-faced, head-shaking, finger-pointing, exasperated meet director, a flock of nervous pilots voicing their concerns about the safety of the day's choice. My good friend and team member, Dogz, looks at the distant dangerous clouds, listens to the childish squealing of the pilots confronting the director, and, before I can open my mouth and start my own squealing, Dogz stares me down, and, with a true and honest tone in his voice, he says to me, "Today… today is a good day to die." And, as crazy as he is, I agree with him.

I am not sure when I first met Dogz, the wild part of Cherokee Indian, part white guy. The man can be kind of an elusive character. It could have been in a bar or it could have been in a car, it could have been at drug deal, or it could have been during a meal, it could have been at cloud base or it could have been at CG's place, I do not like speeding tickets and spam, I do not like them, the man I am. Now I remember: it was a drug deal. I was all fucked up and Dogz was all fucked up and we carried on through the night, writing our names in white powder on a large mirror with a razor blade, snorting the letters away one by one. Dogz is one of a kind. No authority holds him. If you tried to control him, as CG tried many a time, he would do what he wanted and damn the results. Dogz's days are long and his nights even longer. He is amazing. He could still be standing as the party faded and CG and I had long headed for the horizontal. He is a talker about many subjects, an intelligent man who is interested and asks to learn of others, unlike our leader, who talks mostly of himself, and unlike me, who talks mostly to impress the girls. He has an ancient Indian look, with dark swept-back hair, behind an intense set of dark eyes, hiding his magic. He can grow or shrink his six-foot-tall stature to fit the mood of the people around him. He also has a side that I will never understand: his inability to locate himself after he lands. He would land, smoke a joint, and relay to the driver that he was under a white cloud near some green trees. Pilots riding in the Mountain King would have to play over the radio the Find Dogz game, like a TV game show, using the process of elimination.

"Dogz, are you near a road?" We would ask over the radios. "Is the road paved? Is the sun to the left or right of the highway? Which direction are the mountains from your location?"

Our constant searching for him was exasperating and it drove CG crazy, and that was the best part.

Dogz had a custom van with every gadget in the world attached and working to as many places as possible. The rest was covered in black shag carpet. The first woman he was fucking when we met was a black-haired beauty; a nymphomaniac, she tried to screw all his friends and eventually screwed up his mind. His heartbreak was channeled into his flying, and watching him during this time of his life, flying into the impossible, was breathtaking.

I remember once, when CG and I were running from a storm that was filled with lightning, thunder, snow, rain and hail, its black shroud of clouds chasing us as it swept down the length of the mountains and across the continental divide, Dogz was a little speck above us, at 20,000 feet, surfing the storm like he was surfing a warm ocean wave, his broken heart eventually leading him 50 miles beyond where CG and I had landed, soaking wet.

When hang gliders race in competitions, there is a set of tasks for us to accomplish. We race to some distant pre-determined location called the "goal" (the goal is where the party begins), some 20 to 120 miles from launch. Sometimes the smartest, sometimes the luckiest, pilot who gets to goal faster than any of the other pilots is the king eagle, top gun, winning a thousand points for first place and the girl of his choice. Ok, maybe not the girl of his choice, but the respect and admiration of all the other, slower, envious birdmen, a respect savored by the winner until the next day, when, due to bottle flu caused by celebrating the previous day's victory, his hangover usually lands the once great king eagle short of goal. Though I have had some great flights with accompanying hangovers, the pain usually tends to keep my panting mouth hanging open like a hot Saint Bernard, causing lots of aerodynamic drag, slowing me down, proving once again the Flyer's Motto: you cannot soar with the eagles, if you play with the owls. Once you have landed at goal, if you are not hypoxic (a term used when there is lack of oxygen to the brain, usually because you climbed way too high, stayed high too long, or your oxygen cylinder ran out) or frozen to the bone, it's time to celebrate.

During the race to goal, we spend our time chasing locations called "turn points," which require pilots to fly over some object on the ground that stands out – mostly church steeples or saloons, I guess representing good and evil. Once over the turn point, we take a picture over the top of the object, with two different cameras, proving to the judges that you flew there. Two cameras are used because if you only use one and it fails, you get a big fat zero for the day's task. I had previously learned that lesson the hard way, as usual, completing the task and making goal in the top ten, only to have the camera fail. Oh, the pain of traveling from a hero to a zero. That night, I soaked my sunburnt lips in tequila, then put the camera on the hotel room floor, and, acting like a spoiled child, leaped off the bed and landed on the camera with both feet, giving it a proper smashing, and then stumbled into the motel's table lamp, smashing it correctly, too.

Dogz and I walk in our harnesses, under our gliders, with a line of pilots, to the Dinosaur launch. Waddling like penguins, the whole field of 100 competitors shuffles in line out to launch. We shoot Dogz's statement of, "This is a good day too die," like a gun, aiming at one competitor after another, the deadly verbal bullets twisting their egos all to hell. The task picked by the committee is to fly east from Dinosaur, over the desert for 20 miles, to the bar at Massadona. There taking a picture, and then climbing north up onto the sage plateaus for another 20, then another climb to the top of Cross Mountain, turning us again for ten, to a final turn point at State Bridge, for an easy glide east to a goal at Maybell, Colorado.

We launch from Dinosaur and the first part of the flight is excellent, with strong, throaty thermals, as many as 40 pilots,

strung out vertically for 4,000 feet in one big, fat column, looking
like a gaggle of geese following each other around the circle, our
Varios honking to each other, gliding closely, wings tip-to-tip, ag-
gressively trying to avoid each other, at the same time trying to
out-climb the others, our competitive drive working to get in front
of the flock. It is a most beautiful and exciting migration to observe. Running out of lift at cloud base, we start to glide for Massadona; oh, so beautiful, 40 multicolored gliders spread out, bob-
bing up and down in the blue sky, like leaves on the surface of a
stream, sunlight shimmering from our sails, every bird headed for
the saloon at Massadona, preparing for the first turn point picture.
Rounding the turn point, within seconds of each other, like horses
rounding the track, is oh-so-scary. One eye in the camera, one eye
on the sky, one hand on the camera, one hand on the glider, one
eye focused on the picture, one eye focused on the glider, watch
out for the neighbors, try to stay in control, make this turn point
with no midair collisions, yet.

We fly to the second turn point in the task, an intersection of
river and ridge, an anomaly in the earth that created a cross, the
spiritual mecca Cross Mountain our next adventure. After a little
religious experience, photographing the earth's wonders from the
sky, the wind at altitude increases substantially, thereby tilting the
thermals, so that each time we climb up in a thermal, the wind
pushes us farther away from our intended direction. Dogz, CG and
I, the three founding members of Gangreen, are climbing in a nasty, raspy, ass-kicking thermal somewhere around 12,000 feet,
when, off in the distance, something flashy gets my attention. I've
been so busy trying to keep control and avoid colliding with others
traveling to the next turn point, that I made a mistake, failing to
notice the developing storm in the west. I'm not sure if the tall-
looking cloud of dust is a mirage or what, because the sky is the

same color brown as the ground. I relay to CG on the radio, "What the fuck is coming from the west?" and he replies, with an uncharacteristic shock in his typically calm voice, "That is hell, and it is coming our way."

This storm does not act with the usual personality of your typical Rocky Mountain mid-day dust storm. Its dust is too thick, an endless, roiling brown tsunami, the length of which you cannot see, and, at 12,000 feet, there is no seeing over the top. Lightning begins to dance inside it, surreal, as if we are in one of those old, grainy, overexposed, black and white movie scenes of people running into their sod huts, trying to escape the horrible Oklahoma dust bowls.

To me this storm looks like a vast cosmic mouth, filled with huge, gray, ugly teeth, eating and regurgitating every piece of sand, soil and plant in its path, the mouth of a Tyrannosaurus Rex, chomping at me, trying to eat me; it's a monster.

Seeing this monster T- Rex eating everything in its path, Gangreen decides that it is time to get on the ground as soon as possible, before we become dinosaur fodder.

In an instant, the beautiful flight, in which our whole team had a good chance of reaching goal, turns us from teammates into individuals each fighting for our lives. It would have been a victory for us, a hard-won goal fought with friendship and teamwork, by a team that cares more about the friendship than any prize. Our friendship reigns supreme and, though no one can take that away from us, we are all instantly forced to independently race from the storm for our own individual survival. Escape means flying as fast as possible, in the opposite direction of the deadly monster with bad teeth, trying to reach the highway, with 50 other competition pilots fleeing in formation, following our train of thought, the scrambling mass of hang gliders looking like a WWII squadron of B17 bombers trying to escape enemy fighters over Germany.

A monster gust front, pissed off and breathing fire, pushes turbulent winds in front of it. You'd think I would have learned something about storms from my previous near disasters, but not I; the lifting air in front of the storm travels at a rapid pace, catching unsuspecting hang glider pilots in the sky, leaving us scared and unable to get down.

Running tail wind, trying to outrun the storm, fifty pilots begin searching for a sink hole, a divine path out of the sky, allowing for a reasonable chance to survive the onslaught of hell. The rule is that for all the hot air that goes up in thermals, cold air is sinking from the upper atmosphere to replace it. When a hang glider crosses the edge of these two air masses, it is like going over Niagara Falls in a wooden barrel. As you pick up speed, about to hit bottom, a huge boxing glove with the power of Muhammad Ali comes out of the river and punches the wooden barrel back on top of the falls; it is a washing machine out there.

Finally, about five miles downwind, I find a mass of sinking air. By now, Gangreen has been blown far apart, yet we can see each other circling in high speed spiral dives, trying for the ground. I reach the ground safely, and barely get detached from the glider, struggling to maneuver the cumbersome harness in the knee-deep sage brush, fighting furiously to reach the front wires, pulling down hard, my gloves keeping the flying wires from cutting into my hands, wrestling my bucking bronco wing as the storm tries to destroy it. The storm hits, the force of the wind ratcheting up from 20 to 50+ miles per hour in seconds; downwind in the distance, through the dust, I can see pilots, not yet hit by hell, still in the sky, racing for goal. Most of us have decided that goal was not worth it today, but a few think the opposite.

One lucky pilot makes it to goal field just in time to get detached from his glider, grab its nose, aim it at the oncoming storm, and hang on, acting like at least 100 other pilots spread out through the high desert that day. Many of the pilots from other lands are unfamiliar with flying conditions in the high desert, most of them used to the peaceful flying back east of the Mississippi, where the grass is green, the winds more predictable, where life was much safer. A second unlucky pilot makes it over the goal field, the gale force winds greeting him at 50 miles per hour, his forward progress stopped, his immobilized body parked in a strong wind, stuck in one place, no moving forward, no back, his glider bucking wildly as the pilot hovers over the heads of the goal keepers, who try to reach up and grab him, the whole mess on the verge of being turned tail wind, giving him a reason to be very scared. If he is turned tail wind with his glider flying 50 miles per hour, that, added to a tail wind of another 50 miles per hour, will be the end of the poor pilot, who will have little chance of living, since he will be hitting the ground at 100 miles per hour, and, if he lives through that impact, the wreckage of the glider, with him attached, will be blown by the storm, cart wheeling through the sage brush like a loose plastic bag. But, with amazing grace, the people in the goal field grab his glider, pluck him out of the sky, and hold on tightly while the lucky pilot prays, prays that his new guardian angels don't let him go to heaven, not today.

The final victim of the storm's assault is Dall, a usually mild-mannered man, professional in every way, organized, educated, wealthy, but bound and determined to be Superman and make it across the goal that fateful day. He is flying 500 feet up, in the blue, soon to become black, sky, one quarter of a mile up wind of the goal field, when Mother Nature's wrath catches him, powerful and unforgiving, she grabs him with one hand and, with the other hand, she tears Dall away from his glider, like tearing the head from a fish, the tortured sound like putting an aluminum can into your garbage disposal and turning it on. Dall doesn't even get the chance to watch his glider flip over and break, his aircraft is simply ripped out of his hands, sail and frame torn away, a bear tearing a window screen out of cabin, sail and frame tumble like a circus tent into the black of a tornado. Only one section of the glider's frame is left behind, a three-foot-long section of aluminum tubing, called the king post, spun around the hang strap, beating on Dall as he careens through the raining sky. Dall floats alone inside the storm, surrounded by his flying harness, its shape a big puffy grass hopper, his helmeted head with bug antenna drinking water tubes, curly electronic wires protruding from the surface, his arms thrust out of its sides, black leather ski gloves like front claws, and legs retracted inside the bug pod, as if in flight without wings. Dall, 500 feet over the ground, his glider gone, falling away into the Never Ever, attached to a thin hang strap with only the king post left, his life flashing before his eyes, his emergency parachute his only chance for survival.

What is Dall thinking? What mental calculations can he use to rationalize life when playing it so close to death? Possibly he is hypoxic, thinking that he can manage the incoming rage. Possibly his lover is driving him crazy, his broken heart unable to focus on his predicament. Possibly it is his eagerness, so focused on the goal and subsequent trophy that he ignores all things around him. Possibly I can understand what is going on in his mind, then again, probably not.

No sails in his way, no wires to tangle him, only one small piece of frame left, he has no glider wreckage to wrestle against, all he has to do is throw his parachute, just reach for the handle on the front of the harness, grab it with both hands, pull it out of the kangaroo pouch, glance into the black, raining, flashing, horrifying sky and toss it. His white, neatly folded parachute, unpacked, into the rain, dust, gust and rust, opening instantly turning it from virgin white to a dismal gray.

Poor Dall, even with his chute opened, he is still fucked, carried off by his emergency parachute inside a behemoth mud/rain storm, lightning striking, thunder rocking, his body spinning wildly as it dangles below his parachute, a kid on a park swing, unwinding from a full chain twist, traveling at high speed over the ground, his path full of power lines, trees, cacti, fences, trying to skewer him like a shish kabob. Five hundred feet up inside hell, his king post the only thing he has to hang on to for comfort, Dall does the only reasonable thing a man can do in his situation, 100 miles from the nearest hospital: he clings to his favorite aluminum security blanket.

Dall blows over the goal field and heads east, over the horizon and out of sight, as the rest of us pilots watch from the ground. I feel sick. Thoughts travel telepathically, communicated from soul to soul, amid all humans who see Dall's future as dead white meat.

With the storm's passage and the winds abated, a search party is mobilized, including rescue personnel in four wheel drive trucks capable of dealing with the greasy, muddy-like-wet-pottery-clay textured roads. The two trucks full of people and gear spray mud from all four tires, fish tail, and leave deep matching gashes in their wake, heading in the last known direction of Dall's parachute. Dall is found a mile away from goal in a divot of mud, tangled in his chute, very scratched from being dragged by the storm through the sage brush, shaken but breathing. His drawn-out high speed maybe saved his life by spreading out his crash; more like a stone skipping across the water, rather than a speeding bicycle hitting a brick wall. He is a living legend now; his name living on in the fabled halls of hang gliding as Kingpost Dall. He's still flying hang gliders today.

By now the people at this hang gliding meet in the middle of the high desert are scared and here more for survival than for a fun competition. If, because of my experiences, you think that hang gliding is always a death defying activity, you would be right and wrong. Many flights are successfully performed by many types of people every day, all over the world, in a safe and sane manner. You can have a beautiful, safe, ecstatic hang gliding career, living a breathing dream. But if you fly with Gangreen just keep your chute freshly packed, your survival gear handy, your health insurance paid up, a lawyer on call, a credit card with a big limit, and a desire to fly on the edge.

Many folks who come to fly here are unfamiliar with the wilds of Dinosaur country. They want four secure walls and a shower, and stay in the rustic motel in the town of Dinosaur. The folks who are still intimidated, but want to experience the vast wilderness, camp on top of the mountain, in the forest next to launch, where we can see the faint lights of civilization, 15 miles away. Gangreen, of course, chooses to sleep outdoors.

Camping at night, no one around, deep dark; adjoining a trillion stars, the sky a round auditorium, stars taking their bows at the earth's horizon, a feeling of forever, emotionally encircled by the silent sky, dark and chilling, nature's silent, the sounding of your own heartbeat silent; a coyote, a crackle of the fire, creatures in the night eliciting wonder and fear for the humans camping in the land of Dinosaurs. At night, drinking is your courage, and close proximity to the bonfire flame is your place of safety. If you've got the guts to walk out into the darkness, into the wilderness with your spindly little headlamp, good luck, you are on your own. With timeless regularity at dawn and dusk, the coyotes sing to us white meat in the wilderness.

In the morning, the freshly-showered campers drive up the mountain road that winds through the sage and meet up with us stinky campers at launch, and together we commit aviation.

Those who camp in the forest, on the top of the mountain, are welcome to enjoy the many splendors of the Gangreen swimming pool. Located next to the Gangreen trailer, the pool is filled by the local rancher, who brings his 500-gallon water truck up the rough, five-mile-long dirt road, to fill up the round, above-ground, ten-person watering hole, its cool, clear liquid perfect for the hot high desert. This one object makes the camping at launch most excellent, and endears Gangreen to our fellow pilots. The crew flies all day and is completely covered in desert grime, dust filling the wrinkles in our skin and every unclothed orifice, then returns back to launch after a long, hot day, 15 miles from the closest town, and melts into that pool with a very strong rum and coke and 10 other people of different alcoholic persuasions, passes a joint around, tells stories, and relaxes and loves life.

On the first night of camping, CG, the usual bull in the china shop, starts up his particularly loud gasoline-powered generator in the trees next to JT, our lone eagle friend, who is slumbering peacefully in his tent. Now, JT's the type of loner whose hair sticks into the sky like he is constantly plugged in, who survives on his own, deep in the heart of the Rocky Mountains, whose favorite nourishment is weed, and who takes shit from no one. Upon hearing the roar of the generator, JT's tent flap flies open and out he steps, extremely pissed off, not wanting to move his camp nor hear the generator scream into the wilderness for the length of the week-long event at Dinosaur. JT, half-dressed, angry, aggressive, stomps to the trailer to confront CG about the criminal noise, and CG, with his typical lack of political savvy, tells him to go fuck off. So JT figures he will settle this problem man to man, the way we do it in the Wild West. He leaves, but soon returns to the Gangreen trailer brandishing a revolver, searching for CG, the offending party. People in the trailer move excitedly to the rear, impressing on JT that CG was not in the vehicle, and that he is working on the antisocial generator. The viewing audience, with drinks in hand, stumble behind JT at a safe distance, as if watching a reality show, while JT, in a petulant frenzy, finds CG messing with the generator out back.

"Fuck off, is that what you said to me?" JT snarls. "Well, fuck you." Then, just like in the old west, JT's first bullet strikes the ground next to CG's feet. "Dance, mother fucker, dance!"

Bang-dance-bang-dance-bang, pieces of dirt flying, CG's mouth open like the intake of a jet engine, dancing a quick little back-pedaling two-step, bang, bang, bang, until the revolver runs out of bullets, JT swivels on his heels, and swaggers slowly back to his tent. The Gangreen trailer sits without electricity that night, humbled and dark, but for the glow and hiss of the mellowing bonfire. The next day, we get more extension cord and move the generator way down the hill, excavating an old, abandoned mine shaft with picks and shovels and inserting the criminal piece of equipment into it, like a prisoner put into solitary confinement. Starting the generator in the shaft gives the trailer electricity and makes for a great place for all the pilots at launch to charge their radios and phones while cooking a feast of bacon and eggs.

Day three of the USA National Hang Gliding Championships in Dinosaur, Colorado, and the shit starts to stink an hour into
our flight. Once again, a big wall of rain about ten miles long, ac-
companied by the inevitable dust storms and high winds, is marching at us from the north, while the international flock of pilots mi-
grates south, away from peril, the boys of Gangreen among them.
Dogz and CG are about a mile south of me and 2,000 feet lower,
the three of us in separate thermals, climbing and drifting south.
At 15,000 feet, I can also see another, unknown, pilot well below
me, flying fast towards us, trying to reach a thermal. He looks like
he is in the storm's winds because he is quickly covering ground.
As he crosses a tall ridge on his unplanned escape route, the spinning winds behind the ridge catch him off guard and flip his glider
upside down like a piece of driftwood breaking in the curl of an
ocean wave. The pilot lies helplessly in his sail, out of luck, looking up at me. For five long seconds we look at each other, then the
glider cartwheels violently, then somersaults, and then folds in
half, the poor pilot getting pasted in the middle.

Pinned between the folded wings, spinning and thrashing violently, his arms and head moving around as he struggles for his
emergency parachute, the sight gives me sickening hot flashes of
too much tobacco as I watch the pilot below me about to die. The
glider drifts down like a leaf in the wind as the pilot thrashes
around desperately, fighting to get untangled from the ruins of his
glider. He fights his way into the ground. I never see his parachute open, and my mind races towards panic.

Over the radio, I yell to Gangreen, "Let's get the hell out of
here," and then proceed to contact our retrieval crew, relaying what
I've just witnessed. "Call 911, a pilot went in hard, is probably
injured. He is located on a dirt road, north of the main highway,

across the river from a pink water tank," as I dive full blast through the sky.

The scene makes me feel sick and mad at the same time, as my high-altitude dive brings down the temperature inside my helmet, beads of sweat start to freeze to my eyelids, my stomach churns with too much coffee and salsa, even though the storm winds are only mildly turbulent at this altitude. It is time, once again, to turn and run, gliding for survival over the earth, following the highway for ten miles, hoping to find a safe place to land and help locate and rescue the unlucky pilot. Traveling along, I live within my head, the scenario of a dying pilot running through my skull the whole time; I can't get it out. Running out of altitude, I pick a nice pasture next to the highway in which to land, and begin cork-screwing down from 9,000 feet, demanding of myself to get on the ground as soon as possible. My next big mistake, my head so full of torment that I'm not paying close attention to my surroundings, 500 feet above my chosen landing field, I am suddenly hit by the storm's 50 mph winds, winds strong and punchy, like the snapping of a boxer's unprotected cheeks, and I'm having a hard time keeping the bucking glider pointed in the right direction. Flying at 50 miles per hour, I cannot penetrate forward into the wind, flying as fast as I can into the gale and unable to move forward, I am actually going slowly backwards over the ground. This is not good. If I land like this in these high winds, the glider will be torn from my grip as soon as my feet touch the ground, flipping me over backwards, cartwheeling me downwind, the glider slapping my body into the ground like it was on the end of a whip. I know that if the flipping glider does not kill me instantly, I will be hurting for a long time. I pray to God, "If you get me through this one, I will not fly near storms again." I look behind me to see if I am going to be blown into any power lines or houses. Then I notice, down by the river, a big patch of six-foot-tall willow bushes, and my intellect goes into survival mode, thinking, "If I can just drift in reverse into that patch of bushes, they may soften my landing and snag my glider, entangling me in the bush and hopefully stopping me from flipping upside down." I attempt to approach the deck of plants, as if I'm a fighter jet landing in reverse on the deck of an air craft carrier. Flying, bass ackwards, pushed by the overpowering winds, yet controlling the wing's speed, while watching my approach over my shoulder, I proceed to slow down my glider, its speed over the ground increases, pushed by the winds, I am now traveling over the ground in reverse, headed for my only possibility of survival, the tall green willow patch. I set myself up for my first, and possibly last, backward landing approach. This is definitely not in the training manual. Maneuvering into position, this is a one-attempt landing; there is no speeding up the engine to go around and try it again; this is my existence, running on pure heart, adrenaline, total focus, knowing that pain may be coming for me shortly. With 50 feet of clearance, the glider now positioned over the center of the willow patch, I pull the control bar to my feet, diving the nose at the ground, hurling straight down into the tall, thick, pointy willow bushes, I am committed to this decision; either the glider stops or I become an unconscious leaf in the wind. My wing is howling, the noise a function of the tortured air being split by the blade, as I dive full on, plowing face first into the tall willow bushes, burying the angry glider deep into the plants. Immediately, my face is stung by the willows, my sunglasses and oxygen mask are torn out of my helmet and I close my eyes, making peace with the darkness before my impending doom. This is the moment when my adrenaline is on full and the mind is quiet, the survival needs overpowering the fear needs. My karma is put to the test, my fate bonds with payment for past bad deeds, but neither arrive, my future saved by the snags, the glider, my body, my fate coming to a complete stop. Hanging three feet from the ground, bouncing up and down with the flex of the bushes, other than the stinging of my face, I am feeling no great pain, still alive, my world resting in a willow thicket, their great design saving me from extinction. I quickly get untangled from this mess, climb to the ground, bend down on my hands and knees, and I kiss the ground, thanking god that I am still alive.

Dressed in my green harness, green helmet, and my green bug-eye mirrored sunglasses, I fight my way through the maze of brush, like some kind of Swamp Thing chasing a beautiful woman in a skimpy dress. I finally escape, stumbling out onto the open field, and wonder what would have happened if some old rancher with bad eye sight had been there to see this monster grasshopper struggle out of his willow patch. I leave the glider safely parked in the bushes. I remove my harness, and fold it up into its bag; inside its vast chamber resides water, oxygen, tools, food, medical and survival gear. I throw it in backpack form over my shoulders, and walk out to the road, flagging down a passing car. The driver, looking hesitant, stops. He asks if I am ok and I tell him my plight, my story of needing a ride to help a fellow pilot in distress. He exceeds the speed limit as we blaze down the highway, not much more is said between us, stopping across from the pink water tank, a location that I had recognized from the air, where tragedy had unfolded just a short time ago. There, standing next to a truck on the dirt road, is a woman looking as if she is waiting for someone. I climb from the car and walk across the highway to meet her. In my hurried mental state, I didn't thank my chauffer, so, thanks, mister. The woman explains that she lives on the ranch across the river, and had seen the aircraft crash outside her kitchen window. It now lies in a field across the river from her house. She called

the cops, who are coming from Dinosaur 30 miles away. I ask her
to drive me to where she saw the glider crash.

Just as we are getting into her pickup truck, a sheriff's car,
with lights flashing, sirens screaming, full of necessity, races down
the highway, jerking to a stop and blocking us from moving. With
all that my over-stimulated psyche has been through recently, this
noisy intrusion is about to send me over the edge. The cop walks
up to our pickup truck, and I ask him to follow us to the rescue site
and help with the downed pilot. He politely asks me and the lady
to get in his car. Now that the dirty cop has us caged, he informs
us that we must wait for the ambulance. It is his way of controlling the accident scene. I explain to him that I am medically
trained and that the pilot could die before the ambulance gets to
him. The cop won't change his mind, control freak, so I sit in the
police car fuming, silent, fidgeting and waiting for the ambulance
to show. It is amazing the way human nature works. One moment
I am lucky to be alive, the next I am totally pissed. My brain must
be physiologically damaged from my years of riding high on drugs
as well as adrenaline. But I am not wearing handcuffs, no one is
searching me for the joint in my right front pocket, I'm not drunk,
my license is in my wallet, and thinking positively about the situation helps me to relax. Twenty minutes later the ambulance shows,
we huddle on the pavement, a short discussion, logic used for the
rescue plan, letting the ambulance with the rancher inside go first,
me and the local fuzz following. The ambulance climbs the winding dirt road to the top of the hill. Here we can finally see across
the river, looking into the endless fields of sage, instantly finding
what we are searching for, which lies 200 yards past the dark blue
river, surrounded by an ocean of purple and green sage brush, a
large white pile of cloth flickering in the sunlight. It is the pile of
wreckage that fell from the sky, lying there stale, empty, sad, no

pilot dazed and confused and wandering around it. In the middle
of the sail is big hump, the pilot's body. Our two-vehicle posse
heads quickly down the other side of the hill, tracing the rough dirt
road that leads us to the rusty old bridge that will get us across the
river. At the narrow one-lane bridge, we come to a complete stop,
the ambulance is wider than the bridge will allow. I grab my harness from the back seat of the cop's car, open the door, and scramble out. The cop tells me to stay put and I tell him to fuck you, as I
quickly run away, working myself around the ambulance that is
blocking the road, sprinting across the bridge while the profession-
als discuss their next step. I cross the bridge with a nervous feeling, my stomach gurgling, butterflies forming, a scared feeling,
frightened by what I am about to find under that pile of inert fabric.

I reach the wreck, breathing hard, set down my harness, get
on my belly, wrestle my way under the wreckage and get my first
look. The pilot is lying face up, a huge bump on his forehead, looking like an egg has been forced under his skin, stretching it way too
tight; his white helmet covered with dirt, the chin strap twisted to
the side, pulling hard at his brown hair, his mouth full of dirt and
blood, a red and brown trail running down the side of his pasty
white face, smaller stripes of brown and red streaming across his
cheeks, dirt lying on the closed eyelids. I dig my hand into the
chaos and feel for a pulse; he is alive. I stick my finger carefully
into the side of the pilot's mouth, scooping the blood and dirt out
of his airway, and am rewarded by the pull of his breath past my
wet fingers. His chest expands, filling his lungs, and my eyes unexpectedly well up with tears. His arm is bent underneath his
body, in an unnatural triangle shape. Working in the baking sun,
inside the confines of the glider, my sweat is pouring down my
forehead and stinging my eyes, I run my hand over the downed
pilot, searching for other injuries. One side of his rib cage is bust-

ed. I will have to cut him out of the expensive harness that is
wrapped around his body, destroying it. Good thing he is unconscious for this. I dare not move him, taking out my trusty Leather
Man survival knife, and carefully extending the sharp serrated
blade, feeling like a surgeon as I slip the blade between his skin
and the strap pulled tight against it, sawing through the heavy
black seatbelt-type straps, separating them from the blue harness,
freeing him from the hang strap, picking up the glider and moving
it carefully to the side. He is still breathing. I use water to wipe
the gruel from his face in the sun; he appears somewhat better than
a corpse.

Across the field, I see the cop and ambulance crew hauling
as much medical gear as possible, marching behind the rancher,
looking like the marines coming to the rescue, better late than never, to work on him in earnest. They stick a suction tube in his
mouth, clean out more debris, get his vitals stabilized, wrap his
neck in a cervical collar, and six of us fireman-lift him onto a
backboard. He moves and groans in pain, a beautiful sound to my
ears. We use his glider for shade, trying to keep him cool, its last
purpose in this world as we sit and wait for the Flight for Life helicopter. The cop, the one who I told to fuck off, is staring at me, his
hand resting on his gun, a pissed expression on his mug, not saying
a word.

The sight of a helicopter racing through the bright blue Colorado sky is beautiful, the wrecked hang glider moved to a safe distance from the landing zone, the chopper kicking up parts of sage
plants, finally landing with some very serious people exiting the
side door, they take charge, we load the unconscious and injured
pilot aboard, my job is over. At the time the helicopter lands, the
winds from the storm are from the north. In the time it takes us to
load the injured pilot, the winds have switched back around from

the south. When the helicopter is ready, it tries to lift off; it tries
to lift off while being pushed by a tail wind, the beast sliding forward, its landing skids sliding along the ground, snagging a piece
of sage brush, the rear end of the chopper lifting up into the air,
tipping the nose of the helicopter forward and down, turning the
spinning blades into knives, traveling dangerously close to the
helpless rescuers, the occupants of the aircraft watching as the
blades of the chopper are headed right at the people in their path,
just before a big red mess happens, the sagebrush tears from the
ground, releasing the chopper, letting it jerk over their heads,
spraying them with gravel and luck. We all shake hands on a job
well done, then go our separate ways.

When I finally hook up with CG and his son, Kaz, we head
back in the Mountain King to get my glider from inside the willow
thicket. Bringing the Mountain King to a stop in the field at dusk,
one quarter of the sun's rays left, lying on the sage, sunlight reflecting off particles of dust dispersed as I struggle, in search of my
glider, uncomfortably retracing my steps back into the willows,
and finding the glide. To my dismay, it is occupied by a thick
black swarm of mosquitoes, seemingly enjoying an orgy on top of
the white sail, and upon my arrival they go into a wild feeding
frenzy, realizing the food has finally arrived, and the food is me.
Running from the holocaust, I cross the field in two seconds, leaping into the van, slamming the door, the miniature blood sucking
Dinosaurs following behind, buzzing around, waiting. Gangreen
prepares for war, chugging down a couple of powerful rum and
cokes, putting on our helmets, our thick high altitude flying
clothes, face coverings, and gloves, the temperature outside 80 de-
grees. CG, Kaz and I are overdressed, sweating freely inside the
van, it is fucking hot. We step outside, prepared for battle, every
small exposed piece of white meat creating a dinner for the minia-

ture air force. The three of us dive into the battle, dragging the glider in one piece from the grasp of the face-whipping, ankle-turning, mosquito-stinging, wonderful willow bushes that saved my life.

The moisture moves out with the new day, the changing of the weather leading to the final days of flying in the competition. It is spectacular, with lots of pilots getting very high with cloud bases at 20,000 feet (by law we are not allowed above 18,000 feet). Of course, we would pull out of the thermals at 18,000 feet, yeah, right. Flying mile after mile, hour after hour, leap frogging from thermal to thermal, the stress of three previous days fades into the past, hang gliders now flying over the horizon, smiling to the future.

Many personal records are set by happy, smiling, desert-baked pilots, exhausted bodies accomplishing distances of over 120 miles, people from other parts of the world, having never been this high off the ground before, none of them pulling out of thermals until level with heaven. It is nice to finally fly, for the view, for the thrill, with all the others who have been through hell and come out the other end, and begin enjoying the majesty of this country called Dinosaur.

Now that the weather is cooperating, fun is in the air. It's time to start playing practical jokes. While eating at a local restaurant and discussing our plan of attack, our first victim is already way ahead of us, opening the unlocked, unprotected, unprepared Mountain King. With the use of a hose on the side of the restaurant, our first victim completely soaks all six seats, causing a splash when we return to sit in the van and an embarrassing laugh from those who love to receive a good practical joke. We maintain a deep respect for the joker and have a few ideas on who it is that hosed the mighty Mountain King and had the balls to start a war with Gangreen.

Dogz and I are on their trail, by calling in some favors, getting the right people stoned, buying drinks for others, loosening up some tongues, getting them wagging, doing some hotel room snooping, any means necessary to gain an answer for revenge.

A full bag of pot later, it is confirmed that a pilot named Rosi had used that damn hose. So the master of mayhem, Dogz, is let off his leash for the purpose of retaliation. Our search finds Rosi's truck locked but unguarded. This small inconvenience is of no concern for the master. I stand guard while Dogz crawls underneath and ties two chain-pull, heavy duty smoke bombs to the frame of Rosi's truck. Attached to the pull chains, he ties a long line of dental floss, tying the other end to the axle. Duct taped inside the smoke bombs are the fuses of large and loud fire crackers. Sweet revenge comes when Rosi's axles turn, the dental floss spins up around them, yanks the chain, ignites the smoke canisters, and smoke billows out from under the moving vehicle, bringing the smoking truck to a stop, and the curious driver, inspecting the smoke, pokes his head under the truck just as the ignited fire cracker fuses reach their ends and go boom. He tells us his ears rang all night.

On the last day, we all make goal and no one comes in first or the top ten or even the top twenty, but we all make sweet goal, finally. Our egos are happy, our quest for adventure satiated, our hunger for the sky is filled, and I can feel it, time to go wild, to feel free to finish this song of survival and success with an encore.

Dogz wants to drink tequila and then go for a well-deserved soak in the hot tub. We lick salt with the campfire, shoot tequila at the stars, and squeeze lime at the moon, then, driving down the highway to the Vernal, Utah Holiday Inn, we crash the lonely hot tub, soaking the floor with a splash fight, and then lie back drunk, happy and relaxed.

After wearing ourselves out, a family of four possibilities made of good Mormon stock, Mom and Dad, brother and sister, all supporting blond hair, carrying their towels and morals, begins heading our way, unaware of their fate. We watch them cross the parking lot, and before they can open the door to the hot tub gaze-bo, Dogz says to me and CG, "Hide me." He then drops under the frothy water in between me and CG. To our amazement, Dogz can stay hidden under water by breathing the air bubbles coming up from the seat of the hot tub. Can you imagine putting your lips on the seat of a Holiday Inn hot tub? Crazy. CG and I squeeze Dogz between us so that the people entering the tub can't even tell he is there. The sweet Mormon family enters the room and climbs into the tub, completely unaware of Dogz under the frothing white water doing his incredible breathing technique. I am having a hard time keeping a straight face, and CG is doing most of the talking, both of us figuring Dogz has to come up soon.

Fifteen minutes into our visit, the family deep into a dissertation about all the sights available to followers of the Mormon religion, trying to convert our pagan ways, Dogz pops his head up out of the frothing hot water like the Creature from the Black Lagoon and says howdy. The little boy's eyes get about three times wider and maybe he shits his pants, the mom levitates on the surface for a good five seconds. I can't hold it any longer, and me and Dogz lose our minds with laughter. CG is almost drowning as he slides into the middle of the pool in convulsions. The family scrambles out of the tub. The towels they carry are not for drying, but for protection from us, as they stumble, soaking wet, for the closest exit. We get it together and take this family's example to heart.

None of the Gangreen members are in any condition to enjoy the visit with the local cops that are about to show up. Exit stage right, leaving quickly. We have obviously overstayed our welcome.

The next day the adventure in Dinosaur is over and we are both happy and sad; happy that we lived through monsters and mayhem, sad that the adventure and the people are gone. This story of the wildest competition ever held in Colorado will no doubt be remembered and embellished until the time when hang gliding has gone the way of the Dinosaur.

by HARRY MARTIN

CHAPTER FIVE

Tennessee

Two parallel 60-mile-long, 1200-foot-tall ridges, covered in thick forest, create the miles of ridge and thermal lift that we traveled so far to fly in. The wide, level, grass-covered Sequatchie Valley in Tennessee, home of the East Coast Hang Gliding Championships, is bountiful with large open fields, civilization abundant, and with no massive mountains to cross, making life easy for the boys from Colorado. Dissimilar colored houses and brown streaked sedimentary rock outcroppings poke their heads out of the trees along the edge of the ridge. The distance from ridge to ridge gives neighbors looking across the valley at each other a short 15-minute drive to come for a visit. Countless species of wild plants grow on the valley floor, surrounding square fields planted with rows of crops, while a two-lane black asphalt highway slices through the middle of the plant life, meandering through the center of old-fashioned small towns, branching from the asphalt-brown washboard gravel roads connecting the driveways of orderly white farms; the whole, soft, seductive scene looking to the bird people, coming from the dirty Dinosaur high desert, like a 60-mile-long, green plush 36-hole country club. We learned later that, hiding in the shade of the country club Tennessee flora, are water moccasins, copperheads, rattlesnakes as big as your arm, ticks, chiggers, poison oak, poison ivy, and poison sumac – a wilderness teaming with life.

Bolted onto a cliff face that overlooks the small town of Dunlap, TN is a monument to the great state, a large man-made wooden launch ramp known affectionately to pilots around the world as the Tennessee Tree Toppers radial ramp. The ramp's design allows for easy launching in most wind speeds. You can literally fall off the end and fly away. The ramp, located amongst the middle of a long green forest ridge, gives a perfect starting point, affording a pilot the ability to travel 30 miles left or right along the meandering ridge, passing over houses and outcroppings, on the wing in the hazy light blue sky, the leaves of trees below glittering in the sunlight. Behind the ridge sways a sea of trees, their canopy hiding the moonshine stills located on the Cumberland Plateau.

The East Coast Championship in Dunlap, TN is more of a party than a competition; every new pasture we land in quickly fills with friendly locals driving a pickup truck, with a friendly dog in the back, or they walk over carrying some kind of hand tool, wearing overalls and a sweat-stained baseball cap, checking on us to see if "y'all" is ok.

They befriend us, stuff our bellies with multi-flavored, multi-colored, multi-textured magical Southern food, toast us, the scourge of the hang gliding world, by unscrewing the top of a ma-son jar filled with family liquor, bringing to our lips an old recipe distilled through four generations of family, people so proud of the simplest things that I am in awe of their longing to treat a stranger, trespassing from out of the sky, like family. Their dogs – scared, inquisitive, unfriendly, growling, then finally tail wagging, friend-ly, come by to smell our big strange birds. Tennessee's number one cash crop is grown in secret, under the forest canopy, kept se-cret by five generations of neighbors, people who can tell a nark from a nut and who share their get-high crop openly with Gan-green. And a mighty stoner crop it is; a couple puffs of the kind bud passed around in a circle with beautiful southern girls, their first few syllables – "yawl ain't from' round here err yaw?" – ac-cents melting the heart of a Colorado boy like marshmallow on a stick. The town of Dunlap becomes like the sip of an old Tennessee moonshine; unfamiliar going down, but when it hits bottom, the heart fills with a warm, comfortable, peaceful, energy.

Flying in Tennessee is great, even though the local boys out-perform us every day, watching us cocky Rocky Mountain men fly as if mere beginners, they knowing of our long learning curve ahead. Like Icarus, the mythical birdman of old, our egos are our downfall. We act like the ugly American, big-mountain Colorado pilots, and no hicks from the sticks are going to show us how to fly these miniature tree-covered, east coast ridges. Thinking arro-gantly, piece of cake for the bad asses, not understanding that the soft lushness of this world necessitates soft, lush, patient flying. We suck in the competition, suck, suck, suck, the flying conditions are so light that many times we spend 15 minutes just circling in the same place, gaining a little, losing a little, yet maintaining the same elevation, riding this little bug fart of a thermal, getting our-selves aggravated, flying frustrated, losing patience, until the ther-mal, full of hang gliders, finally picks up momentum, its soft ener-gy getting you high enough to glide to the next bug fart. With no stronger lift, we lose patience; it's like trying to get drunk on Coors Light when you're accustomed to Tennessee moonshine. We find ourselves on the floor of lush green Tennessee valley, sadly short of goal, on a painfully regular basis. Little do we understand that we are the hicks: our egos crushed, underwear chafed, and gener-ally pissed off.

Worst of all is when local beginner pilots smirk at us as they land at goal; when we are driving into the goal field instead of fly-ing in, all our gliders tied to the roof of the van, our stressed-out psyches ready to bite off anyone's head who asks, "How'd y'all do?"

So, in a fit of frustration, Gangreen starts to party hard: rum and Cokes, Tennessee fire water chugged out of a canning jar, a big, fat, tasty Tornado Alley joint, routing our frustrations at other pilots, using our favorite semi-lethal weapon, the King Kong water balloon projectile launcher. Planned by our own Cherokee Indian ambushes – dirty ambushes, ambushes on unsuspecting white men – these minor skirmishes help release our frustrations, surprising our victims, soaking them thoroughly, bringing crazed war cry laughter to the escaping tribe in green, a tribe who should not be driving the van.

One night, we prepare, pre-plan, and pre-loaded in a dark field, hidden across an alley from the local hotel, pitting King Kong against Dinosaur's now-legendary King Post Dall. CG and I stack loads of H2O ammo – cold, tight water balloons in our gang's signature green – making ready for King Kong, the great-granddaddy of all water balloon launchers: one serious piece of fun made out of ¾" rubber surgical tubing, it takes three people to operate the gigantic slingshot, one person on each side of the V, arms outstretched, white-knuckling the handles, kneeling for strength against massive stretch, the triggerman pulling back the tubing a good six feet, to the point where it is pulling the others back, the diaper fitted with a green, hydrometric weapon accurate at 50 yards airborne. Here we stalk our prey.

Across the alley, Dogz slithers up to Dall's first floor hotel room door, knocks and runs away. King Kong, in full stretch, aims for the peep hole in the three by eight-foot target. The door opens up and, oh shit, a civilian, fat old man with tits in a wife-beater T-shirt, beer can in hand, wrong door, abort mission, abort, abort!

CG stops just in time, before King Kong can take out a good ol' local and wind Gangreen up in the town hoosegow. We kneel down in the field, trying to hide, watched the old man put on his glasses, scratch his tits and take a pull from his beer can, giving our grassy hiding place the once over. Like three candles on a birthday cake we are; I think he needs new glasses. He, at least, not understanding what those unfamiliar objects are, laying out in that dark field, on the verge of entering him into his first and last wet T-shirt contest. A few minutes go by and he re-enters his hotel room, still scratching, and closes the door. Boy that was close. We need to get this balloon to the right victim in short order, before the old man calls the cops. Dogz comes back to our hiding place, wondering what's up.

"Hey, you picked the wrong victim. It's the second door from the other right. Go try again."

This time Dogz knocks on the right door, King Post Dall's door, a knocking that we, as a team, will regret in the future, but for which we live for right now, the feeling of instant gratification, of releasing some of the insanity that lives inside our bones. We have King Kong ready, as poor Dall, dead to rights, opens his door. CG, the triggerman, yells fire and Dall looks our way, seeing the balloon tear through the sky. Possibly awoken from a nap, his re-actions are too slow; he gets his door only half closed as the mean green projectile hits its mark. A perfect shot striking the half-open hotel door just in front of Dall, the high-velocity balloon exploding like an ocean wave, jerking the door from Dall's hand, spraying him backward into his hotel room, landing him on his ass with a splash. Dall's reactions, as we know from his parachute ride in Dinosaur, are usually very quick, and he is obviously now fully awake in no time, up and running, crossing the hotel parking lot like a hot cannon ball, entering the dark field wearing soaking wet boxer shorts, barefoot, water streaming from his T-shirt, ready to kill. I was expecting Dall, who is a respectable doctor, to have a casual approach to this situation, but as he bears down on us, eyes glowing in rage, his unprofessional vocabulary ("I am going to kill you motherfuckers!") causing us anxiety attacks, I realize that getting caught by the irate doctor will mean our bleeding and needing another doctor. So we jump in the Mountain King and mow down the lush green grass, spinning tires and getting the hell out of the field, leaving a cache of guilty green water balloons in our wake. The next day, Gangreen, hiding behind mirrored green sunglasses, moonshine headaches, cotton mouth, bad breath, and a case of guilt, stumbles uncomfortably close, but not too close, to Dall. Dall acts like he carries no malicious thoughts, nothing is out of the ordinary, no blood no foul; it scares us. How can we know the sheer extent of his desire for revenge, the other team's deviousness, their brilliance, their sights set on the presently unmolested Gangreen?

The day goes by with good flying, no incidents, completely dry, no one taking revenge... but we are definitely looking over our shoulders. The following day, the meet director announces that there will be team pictures taken out on the world-famous Tennessee Tree Toppers launch ramp. This perfectly designed hang glider launch, shaped like the top of an airplane wing, starts off an a flat plane, level with the ground, then slowly tilts down, finally rolling over the front edge. The front edge, where hang glider pilots run from the ramp, throwing themselves out into the sky, is designed for one-way travel, built plenty wide to accommodate the team pilots, running off the end, the only route of escape. The first team struts out on the ramp, posing for the nice folks with cameras, lots of cameras, capturing the event. This is done twice more so that it is looking official, fooling us fools.

In the meantime, General CG orders us to adorn ourselves in nice flying uniforms, dressing us up for a good showing, preparing us for our turn to get on the ramp. People from far and wide have gathered, acting like people rushing to take a picture of Gangreen, unknown militia surrounding the ramp. With Dall spearheading

the center, and everyone else flanking us on both sides, covering
our escape, it is a plan that not even Gangreen could have designed
better. I should have seen the signs of a classic military maneuver,
a half circle with the main thrust centered. There, hidden behind
the group of photographers, is the arsenal: an overpopulation of
garbage cans, strategically placed in the crowd, filled with dirty
trash water, water balloons, and revenge. Total genius. We preen
for our pictures, thinking we are studs, heroes, loved, respected,
beautiful, led by the nose like a pack horse, doing as we are told,
the photographers a human wall, now only one way to escape the
ramp: off the end to certain death.

The meet director, Trick, has the three of us kneel for a classic picture, getting the trees in the background. A farce, this position, used only to slow our escape. The enemy must have planned
this offensive well into a case of liquor, coughing up some great
laughs at our expense.

With Dall as their spearhead, they move slowly, carefully,
dastardly- bastardly, having practiced this maneuver, timing it perfectly. The crowd shuffles around properly, letting the battalion of
weapons advance forward three infantrymen per can, three green,
plastic, dirty, filled-with-cold-water garbage cans, the soldiers taking up positions near the front, while the rear guard fills their arms
with water balloons. Gangreen still preening and posing for every
photo, a portrait of vanity, ignorance and ego, wondering to this
day how many were actually pushing the button, the photographers
were acting so perfectly, giving no indication that we are fucked.
At the exact same time, as if in a military marching drill, the front
line parts, the artillery advances on the ramp, firing quickly, accu-
rately, all three streams of water coming together, making a wave
from three cans of dirty garbage water, the shit flying at our
stunned, gaping, opened mouths, tasting gross, looking disgusting,

smelling stinky, designed perfectly. Pieces of who-knows-what in
our mouths, hair, our fine-looking defiled uniforms done for, the
act feeling like rape. Shocked and defenseless, surrounded by the
enemy, pinned on the ramp, like a parting of the seas, the front line
of photographers, as planned, opens up, leaving us a path for escape, and Gangreen runs, splashing, from the ramp, aiming blindly
for the openings, the laughing natives in the rear ready for us, water balloons, point blank, thrown overhand, like a baseball pitcher,
raining down upon us, increasing our punishment and humiliation.
We look and stink like garbage, our fancy green flight suits, which
match our fancy billboard gliders, which General CG had ordered
us to wear for pictures, are now brown and destroyed, our stench
permeating the van. There is not enough alcohol that night to
clean this blunder from our souls, but we had it coming and it was
beautiful. Turning the tables on us is the highlight of the next
day's pilot meeting, and we stand at attention, taking it like the
bamboozled.

From a long and eventful past, the crew of pilots from Tennessee have called themselves, and for good reason, the Tennessee
Tree Toppers. As they say in Tennessee, there are two kinds of
pilots: ones that have landed in the trees, and ones that are going
to land in the trees. From that statement forward, we are cultured
on the need to carry dental floss in our survival gear, not as a tool
for dental hygiene, but as string for spooling down to a rescue crew
at the base of the tree, attaching it to a rope that then can be hoisted
up for the rescue of sassy Yankees. Although we try, we never
coax this rescue dental floss into anything other than for picking
teeth. But a pilot from Colorado, known as Triss, a man of professional integrity, a United Airlines captain, a member of the prestigious US Hang Gliding Team, the owner of a company that recently

created a revolutionary new glider design, shows us what unbridled competitive intensity means, pushing his competitive will past reason, turning hang gliding into a death-defying circus feat we hope to never see again.

Triss ranks in the top ten for the competition and is desperate to move up to first. The late afternoon sky is already beginning to darken and still Triss is up in the air, trying to complete the day's long task. He is making his final approach, gliding into a first place goal. On the ground in the Mountain King, following behind Triss, cheering him on to victory, is Gangreen, placed in the bottom ten, loaded on rum and Coke, enjoying America's favorite pastime, drinking and driving. One of our own is about to become a hero and we, his chase crew, are excited. Suddenly, unexpectedly, the sky lights up with a bright blue light. Not the customary white lightning flash, but a blue electrical burst that sends waves of panic through the dusky trees. Immediately, the party ends, the rescue starts, everyone instinctively knowing that all is not well on the horizon. We race down the road in the direction of the blue burst, disregarding stop signs and other vehicles, coming upon a heavy set of bouncing power lines crossing over the road, the thick black cables barely visible in the gray sky. Leaving the pavement, we followed the electrical lines. CG is driving the Mountain King, his mind set, unconcerned with fences and foliage, racing forward, dodging the largest objects, his steering wheel rotating back and forth, rear tires fishtailing in sequence, sliding, spinning, treating the grass like driving on ice, the four wheel drive leaving muddy snake prints in his wake as the monster van trespasses from electric tower to electric tower. The Mountain King comes to an abrupt halt in view of the disaster. Gangreen quickly jumps out, ready to assist, yet stands a safe distance from the bouncing cables, contemplating the future of the hanging pilot, sadly accepting the fact

that there is nothing we can do, we can't just pull the electrical
plug, we can't throw him a rope because the rope's connection to
the ground would create an electrical circuit, we can't lean a ladder
up, and time for the dental floss trick is gone. Triss is stuck to the
power lines, his glider hitched to one of the lower lines in the
five-strand set, the melting glider hanging over one side of the cable, his body over the other, both objects balanced equal across the
cable like a scale measuring his fate out correspondingly. The
twanging sound of the five cables moving up and down, looking
like banjo strings playing the theme song to the movie Deliver-
ance, and poor Triss, emotionally involved with the power lines,
bouncing helplessly along with the rhythm. The unfortunate man's
fate is in front of the judge, his verdict due in the next 60 seconds,
a very long time for a decision, a very short time in a man's life,
we stand there soberly, wondering what the decision will be; a
shovel of dirt or a shot of celebration. Triss hasn't just found a few
little neighborhood power lines; no, this is one of the big mothers,
with 5"-thick black cables stretched hundreds of feet between tall
complex towers, the flexing cables containing enough juice to
power five thousand homes, with enough juice left over to spark
large bright blue warning flashes when contacted by an unidenti-
fied flying object.

Triss and his glider bounce in the slackened cables, just waiting for thousands of volts of electricity to release its venom
through his body. We watch as he and his glider trampoline into
the sky and then gravity takes over, sending the whole mess down
to within 20 feet of life. It looks and feels like murder, our heads
nodding up and down with every bounce of the cables, the gathered crowd watching in silence, our minds wondering what Triss is
feeling when his cable stretches as close to the ground as the ten-
sile strength of rubber will allow. I can guess what he is thinking

as he reaches the lowest point in his ride: at this distance, I can fall away, breaking my body against the ground, if my other choice is 50,000 volts. The glider pinning Triss to his future was designed by him, built by him, its revolutionary frame tubing made of a space-age carbon fiber material, as strong as steel yet flexible like fiberglass, woven black plastic fabric that melts under high voltage, a fact missing from the glider's design manual. Long strips of burning molten carbon, resembling flowing lava, start falling from the ends of his wing, and, as if that is not enough, his plastic wing fabric begins to glow and smolder, the bouncing light and dripping lava reflected off the surrounding forest looking like a traveling volcano. We watch the glider burn, hear the molten carbon fiber fall to the ground – zip, zip, zip – and Triss, bouncing away, struggling to get free of his harness, his helmeted head swinging around, looking for freedom, his arms fighting to get loose, his body language communicating clearly that he doesn't know what he's going to do if he does manage to free himself from the glider. At the bottom of another cable stretch, he turns his helmet and looks me in the eye. My stomached drops, my hair stands up on the crack of my life, a pulsing, sickening, hopeless feeling enters through my pores and tear ducts as my soul screeches across a chalk board. Triss's eyes search those on the ground for his wife, knowing that we could be the last people on this earth he will see, and we stand helpless, tears falling for freedom. He heads vertically for another round, his body still thrashing around, searching for anything with which to set himself free. I cover my tears with my hand and pray, "Oh, god, let the horror stop." As he falls to the bottom of the next trough, the cable sagging closest to the ground, Triss slices wildly at the wreckage with his survival knife, flames reflected in the blade. As the cable bottoms out 20 feet from the ground, Triss cuts himself loose, free-falling through the lava and landing like a flopping fish on a pier, then rolling his body across the grass to extinguish his burning harness. Ecstatic relief and pleasure, from heartfelt terror to freedom from pain in 20 feet, such is the demented life of a hang glider pilot. We help Triss tear away from his harness, help him up and dust him off, finger by finger, carefully pulling the gloves from his burnt hands then covering them with ice. His only noticeable pain so far, his hands, burned either by electricity or melting carbon fiber, the ugly burns not causing him enough pain to stop him from holding his wife. I think that maybe while Triss was playing around up there with those cables, he may have seen God. Many new wrinkles crease his face, his eyes, bulging, are open about twice their normal size, the pupils reflecting the still-running zip-zip-zip of the lava. From the faces of the witnesses, standing in the darkness on that Tennessee field, tears and laughter flow freely. We load him in a truck, sending him to the doc. He ends up with some burns on his hands, a good sense of landing before sunset, and a healthy respect for his electric bill. After that act, he earns a free honorary membership in Gangreen.

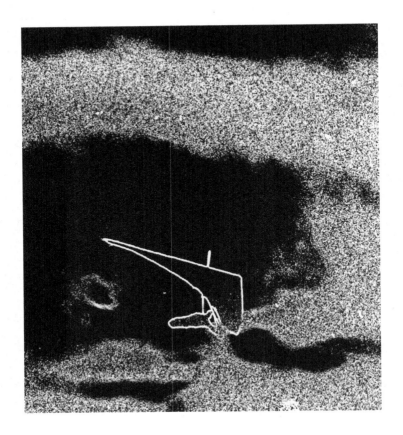

CHAPTER SIX

The Litigated Zone

Gangreen had no type of rigid team structure. We were organized more like the human body.

CG liked being the head, acting like the brains inside the skull, giving orders, and because he had invested the cash, his return was watching the antics performed by me and Dogz. He found his mouth useless, though, learning early on that using words to try and control me and Dogz was like trying to wash a cat. I played the torso, my responsibility keeping the heart beating, accountable for our safety, keeping our team's body from bleeding out, sharing with the team words of caution, like, "Run away, that's a cop!", "Throw your chute!", "Use a rubber," – statements your mother used, statements that mostly went unheeded. Dogz was definitely the legs, relentlessly running off in search of adventure, pushing to the edge of extreme, and then jumping off and dragging us with him. Pilots who represented the team's other body parts, like arms, hands and feet, would come and go over the years. The arms were always helpful for doing the team's heavy lifting, keeping the enemy away. The hands were multifaceted, handling the team's finer details and, when in trouble, dialing for help, but, feet, well, we all knew where they stood, always complaining about everything and that they carried the weight of the whole team, their only concern was with me, myself and I. All of the body parts were needed to fly, except the feet; once the body left the ground, the feet were unnecessary, and the pilots who acted like feet were dropped from the team at the local kiddie pool, where they played with themselves.

The personalities that survived Gangreen could participate in the fly-all-day, party-all-night routine, a mentally degrading and dangerous existence. Tough pilots lasted a month, wild pilots lasted a summer, crazy pilots lasted years. Some pilots fell by the wayside because birds are free and being controlled by another person is not what some people do well. You transformed for the good of the team, like it or not, such as wearing the team uniforms, getting equipment ready, acquiring controlled substances, doing what was asked of you. Sleeping with a teammate's girl was optional. Being a carpenter by trade and a friend by nature, I was dragged by loyalty into finishing an office building for CG, a responsibility that another of CG's friends had walked away from.

CG is not that hard to work for if you can pin him down to his words, like a wrestler pins his opponent. He had no idea of the lunacy of his words when he walked up to me, out of the blue, and announced that he had just signed us up to fly in an international hang gliding competition in the jungles of Brazil.

Figuring we need some help with this adventure, we call up a couple of fellow pilots whose qualifications to join Gangreen are construction skills to finish the office building, able to hold their liquor, roll a good joint, fly cross-country and not complain. Our next challenge includes interviewing potential teammates, finishing the construction on time, putting together all the gear, hang glide locally, and party. Our research on Brazil – a map and picture taken from an airplane of the area – is faxed to CG's office. We wait around the fax machine for it – CG, Dogz, Kaz and myself. Kaz is CG's son, our faithful driver, who left for the jungles as a boy, and returned a hung-over man. The picture spit from the fax shows the smooth face of jungle canopy, wrinkled unevenly by a few dirt roads, pimples of very small towns randomly set in the jungle, the mouth of the large river getting kicked aside by a mean granite rock that pretends to be mountain, the river sweeping past the town of Governador Valadares. Our first viewing of the unfamiliar map pulls our eyes immediately to the top, showing not far from town, flowing on the same river, a large boxed-in section of Brazil bordered by a thick red line, inside of which is written in threatening blood red letters, declaring for all the world to see, this place is the LITIGATED ZONE.

"What does that mean, CG? Is that where the cannibals live?"

A quick e-mail and a few jokes lead us to the answer we want unanswered. "Yes, the cannibals eat in the Litigated Zone, and we taste just like chicken." Our fears distort into humor: our shrunken heads will need smaller helmets, yum white meat, just flew in for a bite, etc. Stop the research, I need a drink.

We will be flying over this unknown place, the Litigated Zone, a threatening section of jungle north of the town of Governador Valadares, home to hidden tribesmen who settle cultural infractions out of court and according to local customs. Civilized laws do not apply in the Litigated Zone. In other words, don't go there, don't fly there, don't land there, and for God's sake, don't die there, because no one will ever come looking for your bones lying in the fire if you do.

But, hey, we're the ugly Americans; we aren't scared of no cannibals. On the surface, all is well; underneath, all is hell, our guts churning as we sit safely drinking in a comfortable oak paneled bar, contemplating our future, wrapped safely in America's arms. We get the project done, the team organized, the gliders dialed, the Litigated Zone branded into our brains. Gangreen is ready to head for the unknowns of Brazil, a third world full of naked women, exotic beaches, fruit drinks, few laws and gigantic jungles.

We arrive at the Rio airport and learn quite quickly about local mind-altering, high-energy, bad-hangover-making-white-men-unwise sugarcane liquor. It is the wrong kind of liquor to be recovering from the next morning, when it is time to check out of customs. We look like terrorists, smell like cattle, stumble on our tongues, barely passing for alive, much less looking like humans. Our dull, aspirin-absorbing brain cells watch as our half-dead bodies drag the suspiciously heavy, 20-foot-long missile-like glider packages past the cops, positioned behind their machine guns, and eventually escaped to the hotel.

In this steamy, sultry, exotic country, anything can happen, and Carnival is what's happening right now. Well, they don't party in the USA like they do in the Brazil. We find that if you're drunk on the local cane juice, half naked, dancing like Michael Jackson in the streets of America, you will be arrested, but if you are drunk, half naked, and dancing like Elvis in the streets of Brazil, you don't even get a second look; however, if you're drunk, fully naked, dancing with a carved jack-o-lantern pumpkin on your head, then Brazilian people will take notice, and watching pumpkin-headed people do this is our first introduction to partying Brazilian style.

It's amazing what a little sin and debauchery can do to cool one's fears. We relax, for now, with new Portuguese porn words to improve our verbal needs, and soft, tropical weather to help us forget the Litigated Zone. Our gear is stowed on an overloaded Volkswagen bus, packed like sardines in salt water. Our non-English-speaking guide, a devout Christian missionary, drives his church's only vehicle, rolling out of Rio at a hair-pulling 45 miles per hour to bring us heathens to the land of cannibals. At this sad speed, salted in heat, with 300 miles ahead of us, the bus is turning into a cheap sauna. Bud, our traveling companion whose similarity to Billy Idol helps him seduce the local female population, climbs out the window of the moving sauna and up onto the roof, lawn-chairing himself between the stacked gliders. I hand him a cassette player, two Jimmy Buffet tapes, and a bottle of duty-free Wild Turkey, then climb up to join him.

With cool tropical night air blowing through our hair, jungle trees flowing over our heads, the stereo cranked up, and a half bottle of Turkey missing, our missionary driver, realizing that we Americans cannot sing a lick, but understanding we know how to have fun, finally has enough, and pulling over, politely asks us, as if speaking to children, to get off his roof and shut up. His stopping the bus to get us off the roof is a big mistake, for Rick, one of our gang, jumps into the driver's seat, locks the door, and deprives the missionary from his sworn duty of driving his own bus. The Christian missionary turns to the heathen leader, CG, for a solution to his dilemma, and only receives shrugged shoulders, CG sticking with us ugly Americans; we are kidnapping this ride, picking up the pace and moving on down the road. A distraught missionary dude is relegated to the back seat, where he just sits there and steams. I feel sorry for the guy, he's just trying to do his job, but not that sorry. Now things are moving, as we get the dangerously overloaded VWB going almost 60 mph downhill.

Gangreen has this trip under control, under control for at least half an hour, right up to the point where we come upon the first large village west of Rio, where the missionary dude panics and starts yelling, "Lombada! Lombada!"

"Hey, Bud, what's a lombada?"

That question mark turns into an exclamation point at the same time we hit the lombada. Have you ever seen an overloaded Volkswagen bus weighed down with 6 people, 5 sets of luggage, and 5 hang gliders tied to the top go grinding into the world's biggest speed bump? Well, it gets a lot more attention than a naked man with a jack-o-lantern on his head. Sparks pour from the front end as the steel bumper plows into the top of a two-foot-tall concrete hump, a hump some asshole built on the road in the middle of town, a concrete monument built for the kids who used to drag race Main Street, the momentum lifting the rear of the bus off the ground, and sending it, screeching, past the shoppers and cafes, where tables full of people, enjoying a meal, are traumatized by the blare of metal, shearing echoes off the buildings on Main Street, in the middle of this quaint little Brazilian village. The bus spins out, coming to rest in the other lane, having rearranged itself from back to front, the pressure of the rapidly shifting luggage squeezing the humor out of our smoking hot guide. Someone has to be, but isn't, hurt; the bus has to be, but isn't, broken. Damn good heathen luck. Only one problem remains: how to plug up the steam coming from the ears of the missionary man. We are told what for in Portuguese, by a religious guy who deserves to go off the deep end, exfoliating profanity, his tirade making him worthy of driving his own bus from that lombada forward.

Six more hours of peaceful travel ensues before we cross into insanity, with 25 days of flying, freedom, freaking, fear, fornication, drug abuse and fun still ahead of us.

The Brazilian sky is misty the following morning from our fourth floor balcony overlooking the gray brick sidewalk, where the street vendors are gathered in front of the hotel for the new arrival of rich Americanos. Across the central traffic circle is a six story building surrounded by bamboo scaffolding, the scaffold looking like a game of Pickup Sticks, the walking planks overloaded with workers, wheelbarrows and gravity, who are plastering a dull pink face onto a nondescript building, the amazing bamboo construction an apparition of faith, a tall exotic tree in the middle of the roundabout, fertilized by cigarette butts and dog poop, its location sad and lonely compared to the tall exotic sea of trees surrounding the town. Fruit, fruit and more fruit covers the trays of the long buffet line, this plethora of fruit and eggs and bacon at the colorfully laid-out tables for Gangreen and the hotel's other visitors. A whole table by itself dedicated to fruit juice provides the perfect nourishment for the dragging travelers. Beautiful dark skinned, curvy female bodies serve us coffee as we try to keep to chewing our food and not chewing our tongues. Do you think we're in heaven? Hurry is the name of the game: get the gear, be ready to go to launch in one hour, General CG has spoken, no complaints from anyone on that. By 10:00 am we have loaded a rickety, Third World rental VW bus with unknown stains on the seats, the whole crew excited and full and heading for launch.

It isn't long before we encounter a steep pitch in the path of our cobblestone road, up which the engine of our untrusting transport cannot lug, so, working as a team, we push her up hill, while General CG chatters the life out of the clutch, our efforts conquering the first of many climbs to the top. We reach the launch area, dripping in tropical sweat, and find the small field on top of the mountain filling up with 120 hang gliders, many of them owned by the world's best pilots, their beautiful, multi-colored, multi-shaped wings set up right in our pathway to launch. This is going to be a serious competition. The sweaty Americans are going to need to get ugly early or be relegated to the back of the line. We proceed to bully our way through an agitated handful of skinny French guys, past the angry Germans, surprised at our gall, squeaking the vehicle past many other languages that we can't understand, but able, nevertheless, to read their hand gestures. We push onward, driving slowly through the world's cultures, until things get very heated.

"Why are you stopping, CG?"

It's just a hand, a bent hand, with the fingers pointed sky-ward, like a traffic cop, the hand connected to a security guard who happens to be standing right where we want to park, the guard screaming, "ALTO! ALTO!" OK, that word we understand.

"Ok, boys," declares CG, our fearless leader, "looks like we unload here. The ugly Americanos have arrived."

He greases the guard's palm with a ten spot, the money en-suring that parking here will be our privilege. Gliders and gear are soon wrested from the van and encircling it into a barrier, protecting our new set-up spot. With our auto stereo blasting music at some unreasonable volume, the team creates a scene, getting us notice for the truly ugly Americans we are. Perhaps our bold arrival is a psychological cover, not wanting any of the world-class pilots to notice that we are nervous, scared, pasty-white hicks from the sticks. A 30-foot-tall white statue of some local Saint is impaled into the peak of the mountain, her back to us, her arms outstretched and facing the city below, possibly to protect the locals from evil. A lot of steel cell phone towers stand at her side, surrounding her like a spider web, a tribute to modern day communication.   A beautiful brown river flows between the Saint of All Cellphone Towers and the town of Governador Valadares.

In the city's center, metallic buildings reflect sunlight, square patterns of roads radiate from the center into the outskirts and the suburbs, dotted with crops and soccer fields, roads disappearing into the surrounding jungle, its roof a vast expanse of green, under which hide my fears, a place surrounded by a thick red ominous line, the Litigated Zone. Small pastures surrounded by tall barriers of trees show themselves as just big enough to get a glider into, but not big enough to slow it down before reaching the trees on the other end. Where in the fuck are we supposed to land?

Hey, we're not scared, and if these world-class pilots are going to launch from this rock, then Gangreen will show them who's boss and launch first, ha. Three thousand feet over the city of Governador Valadares, Brazil stands the lone mountain, the glowing brown river, its surface streaked shiny with pollutants from the upstream steel mills, landing fields in town surrounded by power lines, landing fields in the distance surrounded by spear guns. Noting a lack of landing areas, flying with people we have never even met, launching from a place where we are already lost, is nothing compared to what is blowing its way across the river. It's like a scene from a cheap horror film, but this is real, a wall of clouds 4,000 feet tall stretching from horizon to horizon, sweeping over the landscape and heading our way. Let's think about this for a minute: a place we have never flown before, surrounded by jungle, known to have cannibals, with large reptiles living somewhere under that forest canopy, no English language spoken in the next two countries, and a 4,000-foot tall wall of clouds barreling down on us. As a famous half-breed once said, "Today is a good day to die."

And as a field full of the world's best hang glider pilots stares in disbelief, Dogz sprints off launch by himself, in front of the huge white wall of the unknown, his lone glider circling in the sky, looking like an insect about to get splashed by a speeding windshield. This is where Gangreen shines; if we fly as a team, we die as a team, so the five remaining ugly Americans, in matching gliders, matching harnesses, matching helmets, and matching clothing, run off launch in order, one behind the other, recklessly tossing ourselves, right behind that damn Indian, off into the abyss, throwing ourselves off in full view of the rest of the surprised competitors. The tall wall of marching white cold front is our backdrop as we circle up into the clear blue sky.

My first flying encounter with the soft warm tropical air helps relax my mind, as the team climbs together in a thermal as smooth as a fruit drink, climbing up, gaining 2,000 feet, right over the Saint of All Cellphone Towers and, hallelujah, all team pilots are circling in the same direction. Talking on the radios, we plan to climb to cloud base, getting a good look at the surrounding country, then traveling back towards Rio, flying over the road we drove in on, in the dark, the road cutting a straight path through the jungle, headed south for 300 miles. Our plan to follow the pavement, it being our only lifeline back to the town of Governador

Valadares, seems reasonable; landing anywhere other than next to the road seems perilous. We reach cloud base, the moisture-filled cold front catching us, and without our permission, it continues beyond our understanding, traveling across our world faster than any one of us has ever experienced. The thick white blanket of clouds, draped over the open mine shaft of the earth below, hides our inspection of the geography. Mr. Pages, the guy who literally wrote the how-to book of hang gliding, happens to be circling 300 feet below us when the cold front bullies itself across the countryside, leaving us to fly blind, and though I have committed to memory all of the important information in his training manual, I don't recall that it anywhere says, "If you are flying over unfamiliar, jungle-covered country and a blanket of clouds eliminates your view of the earth, leaving you panicked and without navigation, you should...?" His voice over the radio sounds like that of vibrating panic, and his shared words of wisdom are, basically, "Holly shit, what now? Where are we? Why did we launch? How are we going to survive this?" Truly, the shit has hit the fan. We are thermaling thousands of feet above the jungle, three quarters of that space between us and the tree tops thick with clouds, a total whiteout.

Misty swirling openings appear sporadically in the thick cloud bank, gaps in the storm that afford us quick views of small patches of jungle canopy, these openings enticing us to enter them, like the whorehouses in Rio, leaving us the choice of spiraling down through the gaps, possibly getting near the ground, possibly finding a landing area in this strange land, dressed like space aliens with sprouting wings and using a weird language, we may possibly get a ride back to the highway from a cannibal.

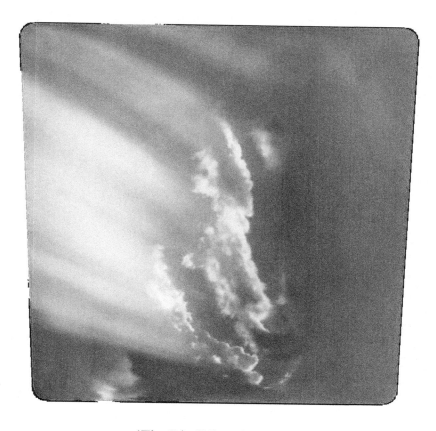

{The Rio Whorehouse entrance}

Oh, yeah, the highway, where the fuck is that? I am border-
ing on total panic, breathing rapidly, my body tensed like I am
about to get punched in the face, my mind racing through every
option I have, sixty times a minute.

I'm not alone. Other souls, lost in the same deadly sky, are
screaming into the radio, "What should we do? Where are we?
Can anybody see me? Where is the highway?" Off in the distance
above the sea of clouds, I can observe their colorful gliders, circling in the lift like a flock of geese huddled together within the
safety of the gaggle. Though I hear them talking, I cannot see

89

Gangreen. I have lost my team, but I have not lost the lift, and I am staying inside the lifesaving South American thermal lift until the clouds blow away or the thermal runs out or I don't know what all.

Dogz shatters my concentration by screaming into my headphone that he tried to enter the Rio whorehouse and is on the ground. In a shaky voice, he reports, "I spiraled down through a tunnel in the wall of clouds.

When I reached the bottom of the clouds, I ran into pouring rain, lost control of my glider, missed the tree tops but crashed through a barbwire fence. My parachute, still in its container on my chest, is torn in half, but I think I am ok."

"Hey, you guys, shut the fuck up!" I yell. "What the fuck was that last transmission?"

"This is Dogz. I am on the ground and I am OK, but don't come down here, it is pouring rain, my parachute is destroyed, I flew out of control through a barbwire fence. The chute saved my life and I never even got to see it open."

Well, that is the transmission that sends me over the edge. I switch off my radio and think to myself, this is not a going to be a good day to die.

There is an extraordinary feeling I get when switching into survival mode. My thoughts become very clear, the usual crap running in there is gone, my focus total. Some people call it clarity of mind, others call it beyond fear. I just know that here I am, and if I fuck up I am dead. My best chance of survival is to stay as far away from the ground as possible, hope the weather changes, and pray that the clouds blow past me.

Working every piece of lift I can find, wringing every ounce of energy out of the sky, climbing as high as possible, looking for soaring birds, looking for other pilots, any advantage to stay aloft, is my total focus. The silent radio and lack of human contact is maddening. Feeling lonely and afraid, I finally switch my communications back on, searching for a friendly voice. I call into the radio, into the scary sky, in a shaky tone.

"Anybody out there copy me?"

I am hoping to hear my mom's voice telling me everything is going to be ok, but all I hear is nothing. I am truly alone, a very scared little boy, missing his mommy. Slowly, for who knows how long I am up here, my overstimulated brain lapses into a hypnotic state, my body tiring, unable to keep my mind focused on the soaring, I begin to panic, again.

An abrupt change of scenery peels me from my stupor, and excitement recharges my soul; after an untold time of staring into blue and white, I am able to see more friendly whorehouse holes separating the sea of clouds, parts of the brown river flashing in the corner of an opening, oh my god, the river, that river, it must be the river I saw running past the city. Shit, how far have I flown? How long have I been in the air? I know I have been heading north because the sun is to the south. Oh, shit, am I in the Litigated Zone? Perhaps I was so psychologically fixated on the Litigated Zone that it just sucked me in. Screw it, if I can land by that river, I can find my way back to the city.

OK, relax, breathe, I think to my hyper-adrenalized soul. Follow this hole in the clouds, get over a landing area, and pay attention. Fuck, yes, there it is, a place for landing, down there, way down there, directly below a big opening in the white cloud bank, a nice green field surrounded by the tall man-eating jungle. Ok, Self, let's spiral this glider through that cavernous opening in the clouds, get ourselves over the field and gently land in that nice big green meadow. I am so high above the ground, and hoping to get this over with, that I spiral the glider down way too fast, knowing it is going to take 15 minutes to reach the earth, petrified that the bank of clouds, like in a science fiction movie, will close in on me during the middle of my descent. Above the wind noise gusting past my helmet, the sounds of my screaming wing sound like a siren, my internal dialogue bouncing in my skull, swinging to both extremes, telling myself to just relax, no, don't relax, get down there, just relax, no, get down there, just relax, hey, listen, you dumb shit, don't blow this. But relax loses the debate and I spiral downward like a spinning top in one direction, get dizzy, lose 1,000 feet, then change direction, unwinding the other way, so excited that I am going to live. Dizzy and elated, tired, petrified, lost, confused, sweating, I make a critical mistake. In preparation for my landing approach, I forget to check the wind direction. My mind is fried; landing, oh yeah, I forgot I am going to get to do that, I have only fantasized of making contact with Mother Earth again alive. Landing a wheeled aircraft, you can roll across the ground at high speeds, but in a hang glider your legs are the landing gear. Using the wind to your advantage to slow your ass down for landing is crucial, because if your legs can't keep up with your speed, like a skateboard getting the high speed wobbles, you pound. I am 200 feet over the field, with only one turn needed to make it into the green landing strip, when my frazzled mind lets all these thoughts come to me, and by then it is too late, the wind direction is what it is. Oh, my good karma, for the wind on the ground is calm. My first Brazilian landing and the field is nice, big and wet. I get in a good stopping flare, but am unable to hold the glider's nose up and land on my belly, splashing softly on my chest, sliding a few feet through the wet grass. I am so excited to be back on the ground, alive, that lying face down in the field, I yell yahoo and, for the second time in my life, I kiss the ground.

Little do I know that my performance in the field is shared with another. Right after I yell, a noise sounds from behind my glider. "Great," I think, "someone is nearby; my luck seems to be getting better. Well, hell, I best unhook, take off the helmet and huge grasshopper harness before I introduce myself. This is a local and I don't want to create anything but a friendly face out here in the middle of Brazil."

I quickly metamorphose back into human form, walk around the other side of the glider to meet my new friend in this beautiful green field, and, oh shit, what have I done to deserve this? Is this day ever going to end? My new acquaintance is a huge, ugly and drooling Brahma bull, chewing and hanging his mouth full of slimy green grass, massively powerful and uncontrollable, the hump on his back bigger than my helmet, his sharp, shiny, horns pointed for my glider, his body colored black and brown speckled linoleum, the kind you would see on the bathroom floor of a cheap trailer house, and his little beady black eyes raises the hackles on my neck as he stares me down.

My adrenaline is back in my throat; he grunts, drools, drops his mouth full of grass and wanders over my way. What the fuck? After just surviving through two hours of pure terror, landing, lost, lonely, exhausted, my ending is to be stomped on by this speckled side of beef? Oh, fuck it, I got nothing to lose. I am lost in the middle of the jungle, miles from any road, out of water, unstable, reckless, completely physically and mentally drained, the idea of making any logical choices is out the door. How about I invent something stupid by looking, really mean, waving my arms like a bird, grunting like Godzilla, giving it back to him? I work on gaining some respect, while hoping he will have mercy and leave me alone. NOT!

I give this monster my best ugly-faced grunt, but he just keeps walking towards me. I can't run away with the unwieldy glider. I can only save my harness. I start dragging my harness in the opposite direction, while he splashes like a giant through the field after me. It is too late for me now, my strategy of not showing fear is over as I run into the forest.

Oh, God, please, and behold, for out of the jungle cometh my savior, one 3-foot- tall, barefoot, half-naked, brown child, the bold soul proceeding to place himself between me and this ugly, drooling one-ton piece of linoleum with horns, the brown child followed by a second angel and yet another, and soon these children are waving their brown arms in the blue sky, in the middle of this beautiful green field, fending off this monster like it's a house cat. Oh, God, thank you.

Where is the village the children have come from? During my terror travels, I saw nothing. It must have been obscured by the cloud bank; I must have passed over it. The thought of any kind of humanity cools my aching mind; oh, I am so relieved, for the second time today my emotions flip-flop from joy to terror to relief to safety. I know from firsthand experience, back in the USA, when landing in an unknown field, my concern involves avoiding a trespassing charge. In Brazil, my concerned involves being lost, poisoned or eaten, which gives me infinitely more respect for the refuge of the good old US of A.

The wonderful, rescuing local children way out here are acting like they have hardly ever seen a car, much less a space man like me, their expressions a cross between "should we stay" or "should we go," happy, but intimidated, the children keep a respectable distance from the unusual creature – that would be me, not the bull, mind you – eyes attentive, feet poised, ready for a quick bail back into the jungle, verbally debating with each other in Portuguese, was I friend or foe? I stand there quietly in the field, remove my sunglasses and give them my best hello, hello I am a friendly space man, waving my hand correctly. The boldest, but not the biggest, creeps his way over to the tip of the glider, giving it a feel. That small child's single act of bravery spurs 10 more children, spilling as if from an ant hill into the field, their welcome presence surrounding the extraordinary spaceship. Terror and panic wash off of me like a cool shower. The children's mouths are clearly in awe, chins tucked in humbleness, as they surround me, their demeanor giving me a feeling of family in this strangely beautiful, hostile world. Using my best acting skills, sign language, and cartoon vocals, I spend my time trying to explain how the glider and harness work, where I came from, and how I got here. We communicate through laughter and caricature sounds, until I point my butt at the distant Brahma bull and make a fart sound, that laughter sealing our bond and our friendship. With help from these astonishing short people, we entertain each other while breaking down my hang glider into the container bag. My life changes in that field as I watch the pure happiness of these children, share in their laughter and giggles, the children unselfishly enjoying a stranger, happily involved in playing their newest game, taking apart my glider. Their desires show in their faces, their pleasure sounds in their laughs, their lives a constant world of wonder. I feel saddened when the glider is in the bag and the game over. Children, in groups of twos and threes, just keep coming out of the deep jungle, and by the time this task is accomplished, the field is filled with an army of little helpers. These children, as if on stage, working with their best acting skills, explain that they had been following my travels as I flew past their homes over the jungle and came chasing after me, running here to see the big bird. Arguments break out between the children, as they always do, be-

cause I can only share with 10 children at a time the honor of carrying the wing. Three other youngsters wear the harness pack like
Siamese triplets. Everyone eventually takes turns carrying the
rolled-up wing, my long white glider bag traveling through the tall
green grass, with a multitude of short brown arms and legs supporting it, looking like the world's largest centipede. The children
laugh and sing as they guide me along the path, holding my hands
and altering my world. We follow a winding single track between
intimidating, massive, mossy jungle trees, their ancient presence
watching us. Long exposed roots growing into the earth hold up
these tree trunks, plants surrounding us painted every shade of
green and formed into every shape imaginable, from one inch tall
to eighty feet tall, surrounding us except for the one small dirt
track on which we walk. All the plants' lives are a constant battle,
fighting for the intermittent rays of sunlight penetrating into the
shaded forest floor. It is probably in my head but it feels like the
waving plants are communicating with each other, silently discussing our travel plans. We journey in this old living forest for about a
mile, the children showing me the way and taking turns holding
my hand. Finally, we exit the trees and enter into a planted field,
where we are met by skinny dogs, then skinny hogs, then skinny
chickens, all related to the skinny children. Adults have been told
by the trees that we are on our way, and come to meet us half way
through the open field, their arrival exciting the children, and they
begin dancing around, telling tales to the adults about the big bull
and the big bird that came out of the sky, their body language ex-
aggerated, hip hop dancers bringing toothless smiles to proud parents' faces. The parents lead the parade to their home, a shack as
old as the forest, a blend of layer upon layer of black molting into
brown shingles covers the roof, the quilted pattern checker board
entertaining a hundred repairs, vertical strips of sharp rusty metal

and tar paper keep the wind and rain from passing through the walls, a barn wood front door hinged with rubber shoe soles, opens and closes amazingly well. Inside the building, humble plywood shelves hold their few dishes and dry goods, a worn but clean wooden table centers the room, four rebuilt wooden chairs surrounding it. To one side of the shack stands an ancient wood burning cook stove. The dirt floor is hard packed by several generations of bare feet, their bloodline calling this small piece of Brazil home.

They invite me into their humble home for a meal, making me feeling guilty about the amount of labor this man and woman, who are very poor, need to complete in order to share their food with a man coming from the land of milk and honey. I am feeling a little out of place in this home, because I am two feet taller, pale white, covered in clothing, wearing a hat and shoes, coming in on the wing, a paleface representing another flavor of humanity and any kind of humanity mixing company with me right now is significant. Salt of the earth are the people who live in this home, their faces worn and wrinkled by life's hardships, patterns of lines etched in their faces, folded over at me into smiles of happiness and friendship. They are extremely humble, yet act like I am the most exciting thing that has happened to them since the birth of their children. I believe that they don't get too many visitors at this remote location, especially ones that fly in from the heavens with their shock of hair sticking out in all directions and wearing shoes. I'm not sure if they fear me or even understood me, because whenever I try to express myself, the expression returning from their faces is huh?, like they are talking to an extraterrestrial. Spread upon the table, laid out for the giant space man to eat, is a meal of bread and spicy porridge so spanking hot that it turns my dry mouth to dust, and unable to hold out any longer, my thirst forces me to drink water from a Third World well. My scrambled brains alarm me with visions of monster amoebas living in the water, swimming in my cup, headed for my guts, turning my ass into a jet engine, the act possibly happening before I can reach civilization for some necessary flame retardant.

I am quite wiped out after the meal and, working hand signals and nods yes or no, they understand my need to be getting to a road, leading to civilization. My only guess is to follow the children, who point in unison to the direction that leads to town. The decision to leave my glider behind is very challenging, but I am too frazzled for a long glider hump to wherever we are bound. Instead, I follow the newest and shortest members of Gangreen, who take turns wrestling my harness through the clairvoyant jungle. Hiking and laughing as a family, we make our way to the nearest two-lane road. Seeing I am going to make it back to the highway, I feel happy and sad; happy I am seeing light at the end of the jungle, sad because I am already missing the people who altered my perception of what it takes to be happy. It is then I realize that wherever I might land in this exotic place, the trees will inform the children and the children will find me and rescue me from myself. With all the day's adventures, I have forgotten what little I learned about this culture, about how poor the people are, about how the school children have very few books and even fewer pencils. So before we left the USA, CG had bought a few cases of pencils for sharing with the children of Brazil. Remembering this, my short-circuited overturned bowel of a brain thinks what a good group of children these are to hand out the few pencils I had buried in my harness. I am psychologically unprepared for what is about to happen. Giving the first pencil to the smallest child, I feel delighted, but my actions unleash the following mind-blowing scene, an in-your-face, dog-eat-dog world, the child with the pencil gripping it tightly in both hands, turning around to face the other children, ducking his head low like a football running back, because he knows what's coming next, head down, his little legs churning for all he's worth and driving forward, trying to get through the front line of the bigger bodies, he is immediately tackled and pinned to the ground, his pencil torn from his hand. What the fuck? His pencil lost, his elbows skinned, dirty tears of frustration running onto his neck, breaking my heart, this is my fault, but no time now to contemplate the greed in a human heart, because the little monsters are surrounding me, groping for the prize, their demanding eyes riveted to the five pencils I hold over my head.

In frustration, I throw the remaining pencils into the crowd. This simple gesture turns the once happy little people into a full-fledged alligator riot of grasping, scrabbling dust, an all-star wrestling match that just grows and grows, as more children hear news of the pencils from the trees and emerge from the jungle to join the melee. So confused are my feelings that all I register is malfunction. I lift my harness onto my back, turn away, and head down the road, the ugly American once again.

Struggling with my blown mind, walking alone to God knows where, unable to go back, uncaring of my future, I trudge through my emotions mile after mile until I eventually run into a pilot from Australia who has endured the storm clouds from hell, telling me his story as I listen quietly in the back of the Australian's team truck. When I return back to the hotel and meet headquarters, I find all my teammates except CG back in civilization, safe and drunk. The bartender fixes something for my nerves as the boys drip cold sugarcane whisky from their glasses over the map, debating on the where they last saw CG and where we lost him. We don't know shit and only pray individually, silently, over the map that somewhere out there CG is alive, and when this adventure is over we will still be alive, too.

CG finally contacts headquarters, relaying that he will be at a truck stop off the highway, 30 miles north of town; he's hitched a ride on an ox cart and things are progressing rather slowly, but he is OK.

I fill up the VW bus with petrol, wondering from where I can borrow another glider if mine is lost. I gag down a cup of ass-puckering brown fluid that the Brazilian behind the counter called coffee, and head back into the jungle, choking away my negative thoughts.

It is dark when I finally find the road back to the shack. The wrestling match is over and all participants have gone home. I hope the family who fed me is home. Yes, sir, the man of the house is home and he is generous enough to guide me to the place where I left my wing, my lovely glider, lost without me, lying in a field out there, somewhere, hidden in the vast dark screaming jungle. My only hope of finding the field, the home of the linoleum monster, is these people from another culture, another language, another world, a world where I am relegated to following a game trail, where the eyes of screeching animals follow me from the tree limbs above, a world where I travel as the prey. Two men and three children enter into the Volkswagen van, my guides once again not understanding a single noise coming from my worn-out face. Using hand signals and basic yes and no words, we communicate directions, the rental van with bad tires, slipping and sliding along a dark muddy two-track, heading deeper into the jungle, I feel like I am in a bad dream, a dream where I am running scared, away from something, not sure what it is, afraid to look back, just keeping going, running but not moving; awakening from my dream, a flash of the headlights reflect on the white cover bag of my lost wing. Relieved to be pulling up to my glider, knowing it would have never come home without these people, people who life's working income is equal to the price of the glider, the glider lying in the jungle, inert, worthless, the value of these simple people helping load it onto the van incalculable. I try to figure out a way I can repay these poor people properly, giving the adults their first in-God-we-trust 20 dollar bill, a small piece of paper that doesn't feel like enough. My glider reunion inspires me to entertain these children through magic. I take a glow stick out of my emergency bag, the same sort of unpretentious tube that millions of American children use during Halloween and millions of teenagers use at raves. It's just a six inch tube that emits a florescent green light when activated, nothing special. Acting like Houdini, I show the inert clear plastic tube to the crowd, make the universal sign for abracadabra, and, poof, the tube glows green. The troop steps back from me as if I have just pulled a pistol. Oh, shit, now what have I done? Ok, make it fun. I wave the glowing wand around, making pretty patterns in the night sky, tossing it up into the air and catching it. The jungle people stare in fear and awe, and then, like a dumb shit, I hand it to the littlest child, who instantly gets wrestled to the ground by his bigger brothers. By the time the men pull them apart, the small child has a dirty face and scratched knees, yet still holds onto his prize with a vice grip. Will I ever learn?

We head back to the shack in silence, the new money family, possibly illiterate, inspecting the $20 bill like it is a small painting. Sadly, I drop my friends off where they signal, on the edge of the jungle, my emotions welling up, knowing I will never see their worn brown faces again.

About an hour later, I meet up with CG at a truck stop. He looks as haggard as me, despite his third rum and coke. He smells like an animal, and is as dirty as one. CG had landed even farther away from civilization than I had, where, he, too, was found by some children who knew a man with an ox cart, and CG had traveled half way back to the highway sitting on something foul in the back of the ox cart, balancing his glider any way he could for five miles on the bouncing ox cart, entering a small town where he reluctantly drank the water, then tied his glider with twine onto the top of a small car (the only one the town had), his one arm out the window, holding the glider in place, bouncing along the road for the next 20 miles, ending up at the truck stop with one arm longer than the other. He says he's never seen anything like it.

"I've seen car wrecks, plane wrecks and bar fights, but they paled in comparison to my surprise of mixing children with pencils."

(A happy family with pencils.)

CHAPTER SEVEN

Her Name is Rio

Reunited back at the hotel bar, our team self-satisfied with their manhood, slurring speech as they excitedly tell their big bad cloud stories, how the heroes tangled with Mother Nature, came out of the battle untarnished, shining like knights in armor, over and over and over, to anyone who will listen, I've heard enough. Me and CG get a bottle of the local fermented sugar cane and lighter fluid and head to our room for something less than adventure, or Brazil or clouds, just wanting a good alcohol buzz filled with peace and quiet.

The next day we awake to rain, a perfect day to be a tourist. Our idea of sightseeing is to search the town for a shady-looking taxi driver, one who can find anything we desire. Sloshing along the gray brick sidewalk through the heart of town, me and Dogz are accosted by a crowd of well-dressed gem dealers, each one waving in our faces a white envelope filled with brilliantly colored gem stones, the sparkling stones hypnotic, their power putting me under their spell, the brilliant purple amethysts sucking me right in, and, like a good gringo, I politely overpay for a fist full.

Next we search the faces of taxicab drivers lining the street. We look for a driver who shows signs of overindulging: red eyes, nervous, smoking, bad breath, desiring to fill his pockets with American dollars, dollars paid by fulfilling his customers' most pressing needs.

Ugly, creepy, dirty, the cabbie's breath smells like garbage, signifying we have entered the right cab. We squirm nervously on the uneven back seat as Dogz voices our desire to the cabbie for coca, the cabbie saying, "You gringo wants cocaine?" and together we say yes.

"Ok," says the cabbie, "I take you to Scar Face."

"Ok," we say, "we want Scar Face."

Figuring old Scar Face is the man with the goods, we let the rough cabbie drive us into the sinister part of town, where possibly they practice Voodoo, boil shrunken heads, cook deep fried thumbs and the like, a place that gives me the creeps, and where, unfortunately, the cabbie stops. He points at the last house at the end of a steep muddy alley, indicating that this is where we go, the house with the windows boarded up, the house that somewhere has a hole poked through from the inside used as secret lookout, the one that may hide a hollowed-out dungeon, like the one in The Silence of the Lambs. We ask our untrustworthy cabbie to wait, hoping a couple of extra bills will work like life insurance as we exit the cab and shuffle up the alley, headed for the crypt.

The front door has been kicked in so we knock on the wall. Out of the back room comes a big dark man showing no scars, his size signifying he is the body guard. Behind him, a scar appears, a scar looking like it was shaped by pounding a face into the metal dashboard of a 1960 Ford pick-up truck, worn by a man with corkscrew eyes, each eye looking a different direction. With so much going on in his face, I am unable to find a place to rest my eyes, failing in my attempt to show him the proper acknowledgement and respect due a thug of his position, so I keep looking at the wall behind him. I am ready to leave right then, but Dogz walks over and shakes his hand, introducing us gringos. He, of course, already knows why we've come, and asks us to sit at the kitchen table. We ask him for some coca and he says, like the cabbie, "You gringos want cocaine?", and, unable to look him in the face, I just nod my head. He returns to the back room while we drip in nervous sweat, trying to ignore the body guard who leers over us like a troll, a troll ready to pounce on his prey, his intimidation complete, our position meek.

From my past, when buying cocaine, I am used to a small 4" square folded bindle of paper with a little mound of powder heaped up in the middle, so when Scar Face reappears carrying a gallon-sized Ziploc bag filled to the top with cocaine, I about shit my pants. Dogz and me look at each other like we just caught Momma kissing Santa, my eyes for the first time focusing in on Scar Face, then taking root on the biggest bag of blow I have ever seen as it travels magically across the room. Scar – that is, Mr. Scar Face, sir – plunks the gallon baggie full of white sparkling crystals, like a waiter serving us breakfast, on the middle of the kitchen table. Dogz begins mumbling and licking froth from his sputtering lips, his attitude resembling a rabid dog salivating over a trapped rabbit, his mind going, going, gone, its grey matter hypnotized by the bag of sparkling white powder, equal to mine being hypnotized by the sparkling gem stones. Finally, Scar Face breaks the spell by asking how much money we got. Dogz said he wants a taste first, and, under the coke's spell, without thinking, whips out and snaps open his knife, its metallic sound bringing the troll to full attention, causing undue stress in a need to be stress free environment. Seeing the error of his ways, Dogz starts backtracking, explaining he just wants to dip the blade into the big coke bag and scoop out the powder to sample the product with a snort. Scar Face is now irritated by our gringo lack of manners, due to our minds being lost under the spell of the sparkling powder.

Scar says sarcastically, "You want a taste gringo? I will give you a taste." He sticks his mitt into the powder, scoops out a large handful of the fluffy cocaine, and reaches across the table shoving it up Dogz's nose, the rest of the powder blowing across the half-breed's face, splotching it like war paint.

The Troll, standing next to the table, watches Dogz's face light up with shock, his laughter filling the room as Dogz proceeds to sputter, spittle, cough and gag the cocaine from his nose. With me, Scar and Troll laughing together, I can feel the stress of the drug deal fade away into camaraderie amongst fellow business partners. Dogz finishes his narcotic-induced epileptic seizure, a serene smile frozen on his face, a clown in white make-up, and mumbles with numb lips, "We will take five hundred dollars' worth of that shit."

Scar plants his hand in the large magic bag, pulls out a huge pile and transfers it into a fresh baggie, and then another handful. Two handfuls filling a sandwich size plastic bag. He zips it tight and gives it to the smiling Dogz, who forks over the five bills and we leave Scar and Troll smiling in the dust.

We strut excitedly down the alley to the waiting cabbie, carrying enough blow in Dogz's trousers to light up Gangreen for a year. Back at the hotel, the magic powder is kept secret between me and Dogz as we gather the team for an important spur-of-the-moment meeting. At issue, a conversation on team planning. Our teammates agitated at being torn away from the bar and the girls they were enjoying gather around a table in our hotel room, for some stupid team meeting. Dogz begins the meeting by saying, "Can I have your attention please?" He then pulls the bag full of white crystals from his fanny pack, drops it in the middle of the table, and creates a room full of open mouthed silence. Ok, you got our attention.

Kings is what Brazilian cocaine makes us, kings of the sky, kings of the coke queens, kings of every druggie that has entered the competition; for the next days, Gangreen has a kingdom, pencils for the children, cocaine for the servants, partying on new levels, flying like Supermen.

That night, Gangreen shows up at the local string of bars (known affectionately as the Chicken Ranch), twitching and grinning, talking bullshit so fast we sound like playing cards slapping on bicycle spokes. With a snout full of sweet Brazilian cocaine and love in our hearts, we coax some of the local ladies onto the dance floor for some jungle rhythm, full contact, sweat slinging, Latin beats. During a break in the action, we find the Australian team hooking up with the hottest ladies in town, so we make the coke do our bidding. Showing the bag of blow to the Australian team is like showing a magnet to steel; instantly, they are on our heels, headed out to the parking lot, as the other members of Gangreen commandeer their vacant seats and attempt to steal the Aussies' girls away.

We continue sharing this big bag of blow with all the national teams except for the English, who continue snubbing their noses at us, the obnoxious ugly Americans; that is, until they find out about the coke. This fact makes them instantly friendly, but we just snub them back, much to the amusement of the Germans, who still don't care for the English, but who love Gangreen. The English are lucky to have us as adversaries, because by two in the morning, Dogz and his bag of tricks has single- handedly eliminated a good part of the next day's hang gliding contestants. Two of the top ten pilots are marooned at the Chicken Ranch by narcotics, mumbling incoherently; eyes rolled back in their heads, a girl on each arm, their minds out of commission. For hicks like us, it's all about beating them before they even get to launch. Gangreen continues throughout the competition to bolster our position, moving up in the standings one night at a time.

At dawn on the following day, CG's brilliance puts the icing on the cake. He takes a taxi to the local high school and hires the gorgeous cheerleading squad to arrive at launch, wearing Gangreen team hats and seductive bathing suits or shoe strings or g-strings or Oh, my god, it is amazing. Each Gangreen member is assigned his own cheerleader, the girls' job to set up our gliders while we watch their beauty from the perspective of lawn chairs, working off our hangovers, sipping on large ice cold glasses full of the local fruit juices, the scene generally twisting the minds of the rest of the male contestants.

In preparation for launch time, CG and I hide our heads up inside the zipped-apart opening of his glider sail, pass a film container full of blow between us, indulge in a few snorts, getting our courage up for another flight over the wild terrain, when I hear someone say, "Hey, you," possibly to us. I pull my head out of the glider, looking around for whatever, and come eye-to-eye with a yellow T-shirt on which is written in big black letters SECURITY. The shirt is an ill-fitting extra-large, its bottom four inches above the belt line of its owner, exposing a belly button the size of a quarter, the extra-hairy, too-tall owner resembling a wrestler, looks directly into the guilt of my eyes. A fighter in authority wearing an official T-shirt, not quite sure what is happening here and giving me the evil eye. Oh, shit. I immediately stuff my head back inside the guilt-ridden glider and look at CG, white rings around his nose, putting into words as plainly as I possibly can, "Don't go out there right now, see you later, and good luck."

I duck out, zigzagging through the maze of gliders, escaping from the guard by hiding under my newest friend's glider on the other end of the field. CG later says he hid his head up inside the glider until the heat finally made him give in to his fate and come up for air. Luckily, the security guard had moved on. If you think flying a hang glider with a numb face full of blow is insane, it is, yet nothing is more exhilarating than climbing in thermals, wing tip to wing tip with 30 hang gliders, their wings spinning and swirling in a dance, your chest thumping wildly, climbing up together, up into the moisture of the clouds, then punching out the side of the white puffy cotton balls, back into squinting daylight, then diving the glider into straight line drag race mode, the wind dragging its whips across your body, plummeting full speed through the sky.

The following day, at the serious Pre-World Championships headquarters, the suffocating pilots meeting includes an extra special announcement, given by the a man in charge, his attitude blasting straight at the insidious Gangreen, glaring at us like a high school principle addressing an obstinate group of teenage boys, making his point perfectly clear, "There will be absolutely no tolerance for drug abuse by the competitors at my meet." I think, ok, we fucked up and we better play our games a greater distance from people in power. Seeing the living conditions inside a third world jail cell is not why we came down here.

As the meet flies on, I begin to relax. The county side, seen from the air, gradually gives up its treasures, revealing big green fields for landing, a sparse network of gravel roads dotted with buildings, meaning civilization within reach. After a nice long day of flying with the local birds, big gray and black birds, the jungle version of the turkey vulture, who drift in close, eye to eye, studying my extra-large wing, wondering what the hell I am, their closeness pilfering my concentration, while in the other thermals little red and yellow finches look for bugs brought up by the rising air, come tweeting around for a look-see. Flying with the birds, and looking them in the eye, watching their curiosity, is so spectacular that I lose my focus on racing and land short of goal. So enamored with the birds am I that I land in a field with a French pilot who is angry for landing short. I introduce myself to the Frenchman, who immediately starts acting cold, denies understanding English, and makes me endure his cold, soggy, bottom-of-the- cardboard-container French fry personality.

I think, "Ok, Frenchy, screw you," but when the French team's truck arrives in the field, I redouble my efforts, trying again to make friends and hitch a ride back to town. But the crew in the truck also acts Frenchy, denying that they can understand me as they spew, "No speak English." It is time for this warlock to cast a spell. Bringing out my film container of magic white powder, I remove the cover and let them all get a good look, my actions casting the intended spell. In unison, the non-English-speaking Frenchmen ask, "Is that cocaine?"

"Oui, oui," I say, instantly becoming their best friend. They want to help load my glider, they want me to ride up front, they want me to sample white French wine, and a party ensues as my new best friends teach me French. We talk of women, cocaine, and their homeland as they entertain me all the way back to town.

That night, me and Dogz, off our leashes, sniff our way around town, needing to wag our tails at something, our minds overstimulated with wild burning energy, our noses leading us across the street to the juice bar, where were we run into the British pilots who think that their shit smells like fruit, and they are agitated. The rumor is out that we've given blow to all the other teams but them. Our experience with some, but not all, of the British boys is that they are self-centered, nose in the sky, we're better than you snobs. Not all of them are bad, but a few rotten apples ruins the juice. Driven by our American values, our need to be the underdogs, like our forefathers, who spent their time aggravating the Red Coats, we begin flirting with the English men's pretty pale-faced girls, talking to them like James Bond, darling. Our attempts are not successful, however, so we stoop to new lows, acting like schoolchildren. We begin shooting spitballs through straws, sending a couple of the Brits over the edge. Our childish actions finally get us kicked out of a juice bar, and not a drop of the evil alcohol to blame in sight, go figure. We cross the town by cab, the vehicle flowing through sultry night, the passing lights of town blurred into a rush, warm sub-tropical smells of moisture and flowers racing into my nostrils , the short hot rain evaporating from the pavement, causing mist to float as if arms wrapping around the moving cab. This cab is driven by a good man, its roof un-dented, a cabbie well-schooled in his culture's tradition of making the gringos overpay. Arriving at the Chicken Ranch, the string of bars filled with beautiful girls dressed in pieces of cloth, any cloth, highlighting the sensual parts beyond the hemlines, brown, firm, naked skin; competitive women's attire. Girls dressed as women, girls dressed to kill, girls wanting to meet rich, handsome, exotic, narcotic-filled foreign pilots. Latin beauties lacking clothes, pasty white Americans drinking fermented sugarcane, shooting 12-gauge narcotics, the stew heating a man's lust to boiling. Exotic people, the climate, the atmosphere, the wild sexual electricity, the heavy boom, boom, boom of Brazilian jungle drums, the lusty music driving my emotions to a peak, vibrating below the belt line, the coca driving my body, alcohol pushing the most pompous of pilots onto the dance floor, a dancing frenzy, Gangreen, thrashing on the dance floor like a bouquet of pasty white lilies blowing in a field of wind-whipped Brown-eyed Susan's, sweaty shirts, sweaty skin, sweat intermingling in an erotic stew of dancers' bodily contact, liquor functioning as a radiator, the bar tab out of control, the team gone astray, the team in disco inferno.

Midway through the evening's activities, a British chap, who is bumped into by a Gangreen chap one time too many and irritated by my antagonistic behavior, is pushed to his limit, thus initiating a bar room floor monkey pile. Where the bar's big man bouncers came from, I will never know. Gangreen is yanked by the bouncers from the pile, a favor to wealthy clients from the bar management who let us escape before the cops show up. CG, Dogz and I move on, leaving the rest of the team to fend for themselves. CG then ditches us by following up on a Chicken Ranch phone number, while me and Dogz head back to the hotel.

Far from going to sleep, Dogz and I need more entertainment. Dogz grabs the water balloon launcher and I get the ammo, dressed in swim trunks, both of us riding with full buzz up the elevator, headed for the pool on the roof. A swimming pool on the roof, one of the dumbest ideas I ever heard, but there it is, surrounded by a six foot high pink stucco wall, which is a good idea in that it kept objects from falling on the people down below. Dogz without adult supervision treats me and the pool guests to a great display of his world-famous cannonball splash techniques, his body running high on narcotic energy, his actions like a kid on too much sugar. It is a treat for me, at least, because he proceeds to scare away all of the other poolside spectators. With the guests running for cover, and Dogz without an audience, our attention turns to water balloons, tying one side of the surgical tubing around a lamp post, my hand holding and aiming the other end of the slingshot. With each step, Dogz grunts and groans as he stretches the elasticity of the thick surgical tubing, reaching full power. With both hands using all my strength, holding one length of tubing, my mind transfixed on that spinal creepy feeling of a broken rubber band, knowing this rubber could break my hand, but trusting Dogz, the master of mayhem.

He lets loose the rubber projectile. Into the night flies the tight, wet balloon, light reflecting on its surface. It passes between me and the lamppost, its shimmering aura shooting out over the stucco wall, streaming water behind like a comet heading into deep space. Our balloon release allows the lively projectile to stay aloft long enough for us to climb onto a table, peer our heads over the wall, and watch the water splash into the main business district on the street six stories below. I know, it is childish and dangerous and an immature way for grown men to act but we are out of control and though no one is hurt we know our karma is going to eventually catch up to us.

People on the street below begin to yell at the ghosts floating around above their heads, their screams searching for us in the dark night sky, yet unable to locate from where the bombardment came. With uninterrupted practice, we finally hit the jackpot, sounding like a bomb, its explosion echoing off the surrounding buildings, a balloon you never knew could make such a noise as it implodes on the roof of a taxi cab. The cabbie inside, maybe he shits his pants, maybe he chokes on his cigarette, maybe his adrenaline shakes his eardrums, but his Latin blood comes to a boil. He stumbles out of that cab screaming Brazilian bloody murder, the few words of profanity we have learned clearly recognizable as the cabbie repeats them over and over. He probably will kill us if he can find us gringo fools. Looking across the rooftops from our vantage point, we watch the flashing lights stream through the corridors of town. The cops, possibly not needing to solve any crimes that night, show up in full force, a posse of police indicating that playtime is over, we escape down the stairs back to our rooms, our laughter unsanitary. After that sick trick we tip the cabbies in Brazil very well.

The following day, the weather man forecasts high winds, thus canceling the day's competition, and forcing Gangreen to come up with another day of creative entertainment. But Gangreen lives to fly, so, damn the weatherman, we're flying. Fully clad in matching uniforms, matching billboard gliders, matching helmets, our matching team with our gliders parked nose to tail like cabbies at the airport, ready to launch, our direction of travel off the end of the wooden ramp. Our first team pilot picks up his wing, balances it on his shoulders, screams like a Voodoo warrior, power-runs off the edge of the ramp and leaps into the windy Brazilian sky. As soon as the ramp is cleared, the next team pilot, running, screaming, follows his teammate into the beyond, the show six times in a row, free and fun entertainment for the spectators at launch. After circling around the Saint of Cell Phone Towers for an hour, I view a fellow American pilot named Champ head out for a landing and, following his lead, we glide towards town. I assume he knows a good place to land, being the holder of the World Open distance record, with a flight of over 300 miles, thinking a pilot with skills of an eagle would be a good judge of landing areas. He leads us to the outskirts of town and flies over a soccer field, his intended landing zone, the big field looking like a good choice. From five minutes above, I watch his glider and his shadow track across the empty field; when they both come together, he stops.

Champ unhooks from his glider and looks up at me, indicating the wind direction, saying over the radio that the field is clear for landing. Then, out of everywhere, as if a stadium full of hysterical soccer fans is emptying the grand stands, into the field comes cars, trucks, bicycles, men, women, children, dogs, frogs and logs, rolling into the soccer field, filling it in, in the space of three minutes, the moving mass of fifty people coming to watch the show, their actions altering my probability of producing a pain-free landing. Panic in my voice, one minute from touchdown, I call in desperation, "Hey, Champ, help me out, what the hell am I supposed to do?" This usually wise man suggests that I land somewhere else.

I splatter into my radio, "That option is not on option." He suggests that I try to land cross wind, next to the power lines on the far edge of the field, and he will try to get 50 people that do not speak his language to move, yeah right. Making my final diving turn into the soccer field, leveling out into ground effect, my glider enters into the field flying straight and level, running six feet off the ground, no turns left, traveling across the field at 40 mph, headed for human beings, strapped to a 30 foot wide neck chopper, hoping no one gets hurt, especially me.

Me and the crowd, eye to eye, living, breathing obstructions, standing in my line of travel, leaving me no possibility of avoiding the untrained mannequins. "Judge, the charge is assault with a hang glider."

Instantaneously, and to my amazement, the people standing in my flight path, educated with few books and even fewer pencils, lie down simultaneously, giving me the clearance to fly over their heads. It is truly a miracle, cast down from the watchful eyes of the Saint of All Cell Towers. I am completely flabbergasted. My landing skills gone, my focus sucked out of my brains, its energy needed to understand this new psychic phenomenon, my stubborn glider unqualified without my mind, piles into the ground. Dust from my impact lifts into the air, my ego put out to pasture as I climb to my feet and unhook. The crowd gathers around, clapping at my circus stunt. By the time I get my harness off, my space is plastered with people, all of them rushing from home, told by the trees to come to the soccer field and see the flying circus. I am surrounded by curiosity, the dreams of flying in every face, the crowd's desire reinforced by touching and feeling the glider, the harness, the helmet, the gringo. Questions about flying come at me like shotgun blasts, all fired in Portuguese, Brazilian people amazed by the men that flew like birds, their curiosity flowing in at me from all points of the compass. By our first few days in Brazil, the word had spread: the pretty, flowery green gliders flying over the jungle equals Gangreen, and Gangreen equals pencils. The frenzy begins. People here and people there, people, people every-where, they commence stepping on my shit and it becomes too much to bear. About the time I am getting pissed, and the mob is getting out of hand, the police, who have finished their report on the mysterious water balloons, force their way into the unruly crowd, the men in uniform wielding batons and guns, very aggres-sively dispersing the crowd, pushing them back like a soccer ball beyond the out-of-bounds border. The crowd, now under control, rings the soccer field, their mood unchanged, their squeals of de-light filling the air as they cheer and applaud each time another pi-lot lands in the unobstructed soccer field. A green field filled with hang gliders, their sails red, orange, yellow, green, blue, indigo and violet and every other color under the sun, six Gangreen gliders organized in a row, and their six foreign pilots mingling in the crowd, smiling, debating amongst themselves as to just how to avoid starting the Brazilian pencil riots.

The expectant children congregate near the pencil breeding glid-ers, the children knowing, preparing, waiting, as if for a float in the parade that is soon going to pass, tossing out free green pencils. Gangreen huddles, in conference. We decide to spread out, and at the same time throw the writing instruments into the ring of fighters, letting the local adults deal with the ensuing fallout. Stupid. The pencils are thrown and the grudge match begins.

A soccer field party - Brazilian style

One old man stands in the crowd watching the children fight, his wise eyes missing nothing, his cotton work clothes speckled with saw dust, his humped back earned by a long life of work, from one shoulder hangs a homemade leather carpenter's belt, his other shoulder carrying the weight of the world, a carpenter stopping to watch the show, commuting home from work. I approached his brown, wrinkled face and I extend my hand to shake

118

his. His hand is strong and pliable, formed by the handle of a hammer and feeling like a well-worn baseball mitt. Little communication between us is necessary. The curious children watch as I hand him a pencil, possibly a sign of friendship. He nods his head, his skin's wrinkles changing as he smiles, he turns his back to me and continues home.

At the next day's pilots meeting, following the mob scene in the soccer field, the meet heads apologize for not controlling the crowds sooner, explaining that it was the first big meet they'd had in Governador Valadares and they never expected such a reception from the locals. From now on, the soccer field will be safer to land in. Following their words with actions, the offending soccer field, for the rest of the competition, is surrounded by military troops standing at attention, rifles across their chests, their backs to the field, each one located 20 feet apart, a human perimeter, fencing off pilots from locals.

Day after day, we drive up the windy cobblestone road to launch, park in the same ten spot, get the gliders set up while surrounded by the beautiful Gangreen girls, get baked by the sun, drink our luscious fruit drinks, waddle our wings like penguins into the launch line, wait our turn and then run off launch, lifting into the wild blue Brazilian yonder. Our flying takes us over beautiful crop circles of green, past vast lonely stretches of jungle, winding dirt roads and asphalt highways, above meandering brown rivers and small multi-colored towns with white church steeples poking out of the middle, the competition organizers designating these steeple crosses for our turn point photos. Unlike the first day's flying in the clouds, the flying never gets violent, scary, or lonely. Way up in the atmosphere, we have companionship, safety in numbers, the Gangreen antics and guts, earning the team respect from the rest of the world. Even the World Champion English team joins us for a climb or two as the field of competitors is strung over the miles. Our motto soon becomes, "If you circle, they will come."

About three quarters through the meet, the Brazilians, not in first place, but with the home field advantage, throw us a curveball, loading the bases, preparing themselves for a bottom-of-the-ninth grand slam, the flight task calling for us to cross over a section of the Litigated Zone. With that announcement comes the raining down of thunder and anger on the meet officials, a heated discussion in half the world's languages mixed into the bubbling cauldron of verbal stew with complaints, finger pointing, rapid blinking, mouths twisting, angry rebellion, red faces, blue faces, sneers, and profanity.

Gangreen, of course, feels the need to spice things up a little. I gaze over at Dogz, but he is having none of it, giving me the crossed arms, legs spread, Indian chief war paint stare: today is a good day to die. We are as scared as the rest of the competitors, but showing fearlessness is Gangreen's style, so, once again, we jump first, indicating to the other pilots, in language they can clearly understand, "Fly or die."

We launch in sequence with a rebel yell, flying on course, wing tip to wing tip, like a squadron of fighter jets, Gangreen gliding proudly away from launch and the rest of the world. From a strong thermal about a mile north of launch, we watch the other teams line up in order and begin launching Gangreen style, one right after the other, one hundred gliders headed straight for us, the whole flock appearing on the horizon like a long gaggle of geese.

Fifty gliders enter the column of lift beneath us, another 20 gliders fly beyond, 30 more enter our thermal and then another 20 streak past, wings coming up in our thermal like a dust devil sucking up poker chips of bold colors, flashing in the sun, spinning around and around, all circling the same direction. Being first and highest in the thermal gives Gangreen the advantage. We don't want to fly alone over the Zone, so we planned ahead, pimping the pilots on the course line in front of us, we let them leave without us and go searching for the next thermal. When they began to circle underneath the next building cloud, we race into the lifting column, entering above them, and climb to cloud base again. It's like playing hang glider leap frog from cloud to cloud, the whole field of competitors working as a team, no lone eagles heading out in front, everyone playing the conservative, staying with the group, watching and waiting, the nervous pack of pilots entering the edge of the Litigated Zone.

Once inside the Zone, the big egos are gone, the big egos are just trying to survive, the big, bad egos unable to outperform anyone, not in any hurry to go it alone, the big egos put on a leash. One hundred individual pilots perform as a tight and coordinated team, even the Brazilians, the all-powerful sun gods who'd come up with this cockamamie idea, are holding back, every wing climbing all the way to cloud base before leaving the security of the thermal, no souls interested in landing alone, no one interested in lunching with cannibals.

Seven thousand feet above the ground, nice and cool, the great height giving pilots a spectacular view deep into the forbidding red border on the map, jungle, jungle and more jungle, no cultivated fields, no roads cutting through the trees, no buildings to live in, just a few lonely birds spiraling over the wilderness. A panorama of dark green, deep blue, cotton ball white, black mountains, a snaky brown river emanating slowly through the forest, one lonely column of smoke rising from the forest floor, penetrating the jungle canopy, someone cooking lunch perhaps. Hopefully no one we knew. Beyond the column of smoke, a long dark mountain chain, one phallic black peak protruding skyward from the middle, suggestive of the King of the mountains, a place possibly worshiped by the natives, but looking like Mount Doom to this white man.

Eroding from Mount Doom, an impenetrable canyon, its walls constructed of high vertical cliffs to imprison the non-flying creatures in the bottom, on the floor of the canyon, survival of the fittest. A long massive chasm; a barrier created by divinity, a natural fence protecting the old way of life from the new way of life. Someplace off in the distance, the substantial canyon drops beyond the horizon, draining its leftovers into the Amazon. I love discovery, experiencing the new and exotic, the mysterious and the strange, and nothing has yet infringed upon my drive for exploration except this one forbidding piece of world. The trees below us wave us away, whispers in the wind warning us to stay away, stay away, this ancient land is protected by deities older than the mountains themselves, and trespassers will be dealt with gradually. What a land, so infinite and wild, bringing me a feeling of grandeur, my little wing, a speck in the sky, drifting over the forever forest, bringing me a feeling of small, the lack of civilization, a feeling of fear, the lump in my throat, a feeling of efficiently gliding to the next gaggle and the comfort of my flock.

Two hours of technical leapfrogging and we pass the test, crossing the barrier, both mental and physical, a barrier that brought the world's best, most competitive, pilots together. With the danger behind, the last leg of the flight ahead, the race back to town is on. Gangreen is surrounded by twenty wings, all of us zipping across the earth at 50 mph, glider after glider chasing for the goal line, racing back to civilization, racing back to safety, as if in the last lap of the Indianapolis 500, go-go-go. We race into the notorious soccer field, surrounded by thousands of screaming fans, their jubilance held at bay by armed soldiers, the soldiers watching the show at attention. Colorful gliders dive across goal, Red Russians, Brown Brazilians, Blue Frenchmen, multi-colored Dutch, the pale English and Gangreen. Ecstatic fans cheering us on, the pilots relieved, the race finished, and yet the best part of the circus is about to begin.

A Spanish pilot, his glider incorporating a homemade cable, is crossing at high speed, one hundred feet over the goal field, when his incapable cable snaps. Its sharp snap abuses our senses, getting every part of our attention, even the crowd goes silent, the soldiers in awe, the pilots on the ground knowing and feeling hopeless. His broken one-winged glider immediately performs a full barrel roll and, on track at diving for the hard ground, his hot Spanish blood on fire, his reactions rapid, he shoots off his emergency parachute like a pistol. His reactions are so quick, meaning that his survival instincts are primed, maybe because he didn't trust the cheese ball strap when he installed it. Take it from us pilots who have been there: save yourself the pain and heartache; buy the best and leave the rest. The flying Spanish conquistador, spinning over the ground, with only ten seconds left to live, throws the parachute, the large silk surface snapping open with a loud pop, the stunned humanity on the ground jolted by the sound, a baby lets out a cry, two more seconds as the Conquistador's forward progress begins to slow, his future taking shape from no way to possibly, four seconds left, two seconds, the Spaniard swings below the chute, his odds improving to maybe, one second left as he sticks his legs out of his harness, time's up, he hits the ground hard, the broken glider follows him in, pounding inches from his flesh, the crowd immobile. The inert pilot is spread out on the field, one second, five, ten seconds, a question hanging in the air, the crowd is stunned, no one moves, his grass stained helmet turns, he looks at the crowd, he is alive, the crowd goes berserk, the military can't hold them back, and another party begins.

Four final days of the meet are reserved for the top pilots, and, sadly, I do not make the cut. I take it hard at first, my ego shedding tears, my soul throwing a temper tantrum, taking my medicine and washing the bitter pill down with cane juice, and then moving forward.

Thinking ahead, Gangreen brought a tandem glider with us to Brazil, so I spend the last few days taking tandem victims for rides. Tandem hang gliding is like no other experience. I am responsible for another person's life. Killing myself is my fault, killing another is my fault plus eternal karma. I quit the blow and focus on fulfilling my responsibilities, bringing people's dreams to life. Going from dereliction of duty to responsibility in a single bound cheers me up, and I begin to feel that my inability to be World Champion is inevitable.

Humans dream of flying like birds, and I am a conduit fulfilling their dreams. Being human, I am not perfect and can make mistakes. Flying solo, you can survive making five or six mistakes, but tandem flying, three strikes and you're out. So why do I do it? It is the smiles, the tears, the hugs, the fears, it is the look that comes to their faces, it is the joy, it is the sounds created by their souls. When leaving the ground, women and men emanate a sound, coming from deep down, the sound bubbling up to the surface, its resonance like that of a purring animal, a noise directly from the person's spirit. Some people yell, some gasp, and some just utter a low groan of ecstasy. I have taken over 300 people tandem and the reaction is universally the same; in one way or another, they convey that tandem hang gliding is the greatest thing they have ever done, and I agree.

My first tandem victim in Brazil is a German girl, not an athletic type, possibly her profession an accountant, the scenario creating a big challenge for me, and a bigger challenge for her, because she is unable to speak English, but her powerful, sparkling eyes and worthy enthusiasm make my softer side incapable of telling her no. With the help of an interpreter, we guide her through the process, practicing over and over the sequence of events. Our sequence flows like this: one hand will be holding my right shoulder strap, the other on my left, walking side by side, like bride and groom, we will enter onto the ramp, next picking up the wing and stabilizing it into the wind, I will ask if you are ready, you will say "ya" or "nine." If it is ya, my next words will be, "Mach Snell," meaning we will begin walking evenly, then jogging evenly, and then running our balls off for the end of the ramp, whereupon entering atmosphere, we will lay down and stretch our legs into the harnesses, and if you have any problems, tap my helmet. Coming into land, take your feet out of the harness, pull upright, hold tight, and be ready to run. That is my demand and I am not going until you understand. Her concentration is like that of a German officer, and we quickly improve her skills, until, finally, she and the interpreter prove to me that she will be safe.

Leaving the end of the ramp, she makes not a sound; weird. We enter strong lift and begin circling, in our beautiful lone thermal, which is not empty for long, as solo pilots fly their wings in to join us. An unknown pilot flying across from us at equal elevation, driving a solid red glider, maybe a Russian, begins waving hello, both of us waving back, the scenery beneath us a National Geographic cover shot, a first-rate tandem flight progressing.

We continue carving circles up over the Saint of All Cell Towers, gaining 3,000 feet, and then she begins tapping me on the helmet, only partially pulling my attention away from the beautiful world around us. I think her knocking is expressing her enthusi-asm for the beauty of the river below us, but what she is trying to express is, "I need to land. Now." My bad.

We circle on. She begins hammering on my helmet, this time shaking me out of my stupor and bringing on my concern. I level the wing out and begin gliding for the landing area, unfortu-nately for her, a little too late. She pukes inside the fancy new full-coverage helmet she is wearing, thankfully turning her face away from me. Her regurgitated lunch flies past the chin guard of the helmet and streaks across my tandem harness, the juices covering over the stains left by other victims, the larger chunks missing the fabric and falling below, becoming fertilizer for the forest.

Shit. She expresses her sorrow in German gibberish, and we move her recovery forward by breathing deeply, drinking water, placing her at ease. I turn her loss into laughter by pinching my nose, shrugging my shoulders, and spreading my arms out to flap like a bird, while she tries controlling the glider on her own. These actions move the color back to her face, she becomes refocused, and keeps her concentration on the now, my goal accomplished, preparing her mind for landing.

Coming into the soccer field, our landing perfect, the ap-plause from the crowd brings German pride to my passenger. Her face is a little pale, but her body language ecstatic, hugging me gratefully and delightfully kissing my cheeks, she walks from the field a new woman, her dreams come true.

That night at the hotel, I listen to the team's rendition of their competition day while I scrub in the tub, cleaning the goop from my gear, feeling like Cinderella as she listens to her mean older sisters speak of the ball.

The next day, my tandem victim was Kaz, our trusty driver, his dull eyes nursing a sugar cane hangover. He says he's ready, and how could I argue? I have spent many a great flight hanging with a hangover. His downfall, however, is bringing a movie camera. Staring through the lens at the swirling sky, while we bump and jostle around and around, Kaz's face starts to go green. Speaking English, he lets me know he is feeling like last night's party is moving up. We head out to land, his stomach still full, and we land to the pleasure of the crowd, my responsibilities over. Kaz and I leave the field in search of the hair of the dog.

Returning with a bottle, we lounge around goal, trying to sweet talk girls in broken Portuguese until the Gangreen boys race in to the cheers of the crowds. It is the final race and the competition is over.

The next day we say good-bye to our new friends, many of whom we can't understand and will never see again, good-bye to the children who took our pencils and our hearts, and good-bye and thank you to the Saint of All Cell Phone Towers for watching over us. Gangreen's competitive spirit never ends as we snorted bigger and bigger lines and tell bigger and bigger lies on our way back to Rio, constant laughter forcing the coke to travel in reverse from our noses. We are free spirits, living the dream, traveling down the big lombada road back to Rio.

The last excitement in Rio is no excitement at all because while I flirt in the hotel lobby, Dogz gets mugged outside by a large group of young boys who live in the Voodoo hills surrounding the hotel, the group of degenerates jumping him, driving him to the pavement, tearing his cherished turquoise eagle necklace from his throat. That night me and Dogz, heroes on drugs, go on a reckless search for his necklace, trying to get a taxi ride up into the voodoo hills behind the hotel, but the taxi driver, with fear in his eyes, expresses to us, "No voodoo, no voodoo," while we wave 100 dollar bills in his face. He makes us get out of the cab and drives off. I guess the cabbie was doing us ignorant gringos right. No one messes around with Brazilian Voodoo. If you happen to be in Rio and see a large eagle-cut turquoise necklace that looks out of place, contact me. Dogz would sure like it back.

We party hard the last night in Brazil, trying not to leave anything behind that might cause problems in customs. Gangreen shows up the next morning at the Rio airport incoherent and with a very serious problem: we have some cocaine left. It's a sin to waste it or, worse, take it on the plane, so Dogz, me and CG sit on the toilets in the men's room of the Real Degenerate International Airport, pants on, ready to run, passing the film container back and forth under the dividers until we can take no more, flushing the half-full canister of best-blow-we-ever had down the Oh, God, I don't want to remember.

The team, after trying to drink the flight dry, looks like human melted candle wax, getting back to the States in sorry shape. We limp through LAX, share with each other how we've fallen in love with the people and the country and the children and, most of all, the swallowing of ten Ibuprofens, in an attempt to reenter the real world. CG and I lumber home from LA to Colorado in the Mountain King, and are stopped for speeding only once.

(CG and his new friends)

CHAPTER EIGHT

Russian, Biker, Injun, Spy

In the cold Telluride morning air, my hands frozen, reaching into my tool belt, grabbing another handful of nails, my feet balancing on top of a six-inch-wide wall, ten feet off the ground, I wait for the hung-over crane operator to bring me another truss, ignoring the cold by fantasizing about a girl who I'd met in the bar the night before, hoping the sun's rays will hurry over the ridge and warm me up. I notice in the distant sunlight, traveling up the dirt driveway, heading to the construction site, a Volkswagen bus with a hang glider tied to the roof. Driving the bus is Rick, a fellow Gangreen teammate, his arrival bringing me news of my future at this job. My boss watches with a scowl as the hippie bus comes to a stop. I mentioned to my boss, earlier in the week, about the US Nationals coming up at Dunlap, California, and he mentioned nothing back, but his experience employing hang gliding junkies, and the scowl on his face, says plenty. Rick scrambles from the bus, walks over to where I'm working, followed by my boss, and all Rick says is, "We're going," and my boss says, "You're fired."

"That's ok," I say, "I've been fired from better jobs than this."

Dunlap, California, located in the foothills of the Sierra Mountains, is a land of hard working small town people who are living there for the beauty and peace of the country. It is a landscape full of chirping birds and children with lemonade stands, sunbaked faces and people who wave at any passerby. Hidden in the forests outside of town, between the round grass-covered hills, seedy bars, dilapidated ranches, possible meth labs, deadhead dope fields, homes for bikers with tats and colors, ranchers sitting in parked trucks displaying rifles in their rear windows, hippie communes, and other good patriotic Americans living here and evading the empire, avoiding the taxman.

The Dunlap Nationals bring in the best pilots from across the USA, across the world, across the political arena and across income levels, all competing against each another on a level playing field. Prior to the Nationals, the United States' hang gliding legislative body was contacted by the Russian hang gliding legislative body in preparation for sending over some athletes to represent Russia at America's most prestigious competition. The whole Russian team was coming to America to fly with us, and the best part is that Gangreen is going to be the Russian team's escorts. Letting Gangreen be responsible for anything is like letting your daughter ride in the Mountain King. You just don't do it. Nevertheless, four Russian pilots show up in Dunlap early in the morning, with a few extra people in tow. Two of them call themselves newspaper reporters and the third is either a narc or a cop, maybe even KGB, as indicated by his shifty eyes and how he takes the world very seriously. Of course, he is their translator, so we are stuck with him. Russian representatives dressed in red, American representatives dressed in white, people from the left, people from the right, stand up, sit down, fight, fight, fight.

Thinking ahead, the Russian pilots brought with them a friendship package, and set it on a picnic bench in the campground where we are staying, with pilots and guests all around, they open it and pull out the mystery contents. The package consists of some plates and knives, some nice-looking homemade black bread wrapped in paper, and cream cheese that comes out of a tin. This is their present to Gangreen, a customary Russian breakfast. One of the Russian pilots spreads the cream cheese thickly over the black bread, sets the piece on a plate in front of me; all eyes are on me, waiting for my taste approval. I pick it up, skeptically, and look around, pointing the morsel at Dogz and CG to see if they have the desire to go first; both shake their heads, indicating, "No, you are stuck, be a good boy, you're the first victim." Ok, I take a big bite, proving I am not chicken, and start chewing. It tastes like black bread, but the cream cheese, having the consistency of grease, tastes bland, like chewing on toilet paper. Yuck, I realize, it's lard.

There I sit, Russians to the left of me, KGB to the right, in front of me two newspaper reporters taking pictures, Gangreen and others surrounding me. The foul texture and taste is more than I can swallow, and I spit the shit out, the black and white turd falling from my mouth and splatting on top of the wood table for all to see. Not good. Have I just insulted these folks, my actions offending the historical breakfast of Mother Russia? Is the KGB agent going to pull a pistol and pop me, execution style?

Silence follows, my eyes searching the crowd for forgiveness, the uneasy feeling persists, forgiveness not forthcoming, the silence of time ticks on. I grab the turd and hurl it into the woods as I figure out what I am going to do to save face. I hold up my hand and signal with one finger, hopefully the international gesture for, "Please give me a minute." Taking ahold of Dogz's shirt and forcing him to help me, both of us high-tail it over to the Gangreen trailer. Inside the trailer, we begin collecting cereal bowls, milk and a big box of granola while all the offended participants wait at the table for our return. We soon reappear, acting like waiters, Dogz setting bowls in front of the offended, I follow him by filling the bowls with granola, Dogz circling the table, pouring a round of milk, I running back to the trailer for spoons, finally the first Russian takes a sample, chews this new crunchy delicious breakfast, his head nodding pleasure, his other teammates following suit. The KGB guy, looking angry and much less open-minded, defiantly eats his black bread and lard. We eat breakfast, take pictures, shake hands, laugh and fart, smile and point at launch, nodding our heads and becoming acquainted, enjoying each other. After the officials leave, Dogz and I ambush three of the Russian pilots and hustle them into the Gangreen trailer, introducing them to a more traditional form of American hospitality. While Dogz rolls up two joints for their heads, I share with them a great American pleasure, Hustler magazine. One Ruski looks nervously out the window, two Gangreeners pass the joint, three Ruskis take turns at the window, four porn mags circulate the trailer, five paranoid stoners feel apprehensive about the location of Lard Man. We finish our safety meeting with a roach on the end of the tweezers, the Russian boys relaxed and a long ways from home, enjoying the Colorado boys' brand of American neighborliness.

Next plan of action, load their gliders onto our luxurious Astro van and drive our new friends, who are stoned to the bone, up to launch, with Pink Floyd a-blasting, steaming coffee poured, more joints rolled, preparing them for their first day of hang dangling over American soil.

On launch, the Ruskis, coming from the Old World, shock the field of competitors by opening their old and dilapidated gliders, which look like contraptions made from salvage yard airplane parts. Once the meet director gets a look at these relics, his concern for safety disallows them from flying from this hill. It is mortifying. Great Mother Russia sent her best pilots to represent her in America with gliders deemed unsafe for human consumption. Russia, with a land mass twice, maybe thrice, as big as the USA, with thousands of nuclear weapons hidden inside her, sent her top-rated pilot with a glider whose frame he proudly built himself, pos-

134

sibly made out of old swing set tubing, the sail sewed proudly by his mother, the cloth possibly salvaged from an old sailboat. The Russians proudly continue setting up their wings as the meet director consults with CG and others at launch. While the four old gliders are being prepared for the competition between two nations and everything seems fine until the Russian team gets a look at our wings.

On their faces, the once-stoic Russian expressions now look like they've just lost the war. They stand amongst their Volkswagen-like gliders, while we stand around our Ferraris, everyone knowing the Russians don't have a chance in hell of competing against us fairly. The situation is just not right.

Americans to the rescue. America the Giving, we fought and died to give the slaves freedom, we died by the thousands and gave Germany back to its people, we paid and died in the Middle East and took just enough land to bury our dead, and to the Russians we loan top-of-the-line demo gliders, making their skills their only justification for beating us fair and square.

The great man, Krown, our local glider representative, saves the day by lending expensive gliders to poor strangers, rocking the Cossacks' world, advancing the Old World pilots forward into New World technology; Krown the Giving, moving across borders like a pawn advancing on a king, forcing checkmate, Krown's new status: soul mate to the Russian people. Full grown Russian men are so astonished by American generosity that their eyes rim in tears, and Russian bear hugs are spread all around. The Russian pilots' new gliders, snare drum tight, the sails crispy-clean fresh, unscratched aluminum tubing shining in the sun, the wings looking fast, like stallions at the gate, are ready to race.

Try as we might, the Russian pilot whose glider involved the love of his mother will not let his go. With three out of four gliders switched out, the meet director is so impressed with the pilot's mom sewing his sail that he reverses his decision and says let her fly. The most challenging aspect of competitive sports is controlling the mind, and knowing your mom put her love and sweat into your equipment might just give a man the mental edge he needs to rise above with love.

Setting up a hang glider is simple. You stand it upright, spreading the wings, keeping the sail out of the dirt, install the top pieces, kneel down under the wing and install the bottom pieces. The Russian pilots begin assembling the gliders upright, keeping the sail out of the dirt and installing the top pieces, and then, to our astonishment, rolling the glider upside down onto the king post, installing the bottom pieces, and then rolling the glider right side up, thus saving themselves from having to bend over, the action not hurting the gliders, but wearing on the owner. Krown the Giving observes this rolling action and shakes his head silently, his attitude patient, like a father watching his children playing incorrectly with their new expensive toys. Me and Dogz like the new Russian set-up technique so much that we roll ours upside down, too, helping to bring laughs and camaraderie to the competitors on launch.

The Russians are a constant source of amusement, quickly becoming the meet's center of attention, our language barrier workable, the different culture enjoyable, different people from different places bringing smiles to the faces of the 100 pilots here to race. Gangreen and the Russians launched en mass, climbing together, and the problems begin early, because the Republicans are circling to the right and the Socialists are circling to the left, like a NASCAR race with half of the cars speeding in the opposite direction; creating political unrest, not to mention a possible midair collision. Let's all be working together here. By circling our hands in the correct direction of travel, and screaming verbal abuses, the Socialists catch on, Gangreen showing them the error of their political direction.

Worthy competitors the Ruskis prove to be, climbing efficiently to cloud base, going on glide to the next most likely thermal, cutting people off in the lift, not waiting around for others, bird men from another continent, dicing it up in the sky.

After a great flight, Gangreen plus the Ruskis load back in the van, tie the gliders on the racks, and head to camp to break out the booze. Gangreen learns quickly, when competing against vodka-trained athletes, we are a mere assemblage of choir boys, the Russians absorbing alcohol like paper towels, vodka like mother's milk, guzzling three drinks to our one, their behavior not slurring, not stumbling, with bright eyes, ready for more; Gangreen's – alcohol poisoning, absorbing alcohol like a rock, slurring, stumbling, eyes crossed, unable to keep up, ready for bed.

Dawn the next day, my head, pain, will someone please chop off my head? My brain feels as if the Liberty Bell was cracked by my cranium, its tenor ringing to the rhythm of my heartbeat; give me aspirin and pot, lots of pot, keep those fucking Ruskis away from me, it's all their fault.

Obviously, the Ruskis are spies, looking for secrets, wearing down Gangreen, beating us at our own game, crushing the competition at night, and letting the ashes blow away by day. Gangreen will never back down, party as a team, puke as a team – ten more days of trying to drink like a Russian, ten more days of my sandpaper tongue sticking to the roof of my skull, ten more days of Dogz rattling the trailer, snoring like a thunder storm, my brain in retreat.

Gangreen's hopes of national stardom, dashed; placing in the top ten, history; the top twenty, a miracle; the bottom twenty, hopeful. The crew of ragged misfits shows up at the pilots meeting, our green clothing matching the green of our gills, the Russians all smiles and handshakes, the Ruskis ready to fly, Gangreen ready to cry. How can this be happening? CG, how are we going to out-party people who were born to party?

As the day's competition drags on, me and my glider positioned on launch, smooth winds blowing straight into the ramp, my wings floating on my shoulders, my body prepared to fly, my brain pounding an awful drum solo, previously launched pilots climbing to the clouds, the pilot standing behind me, happy and healthy, excited to go flying, his mom has sewn his sail, his mom is an alcoholic.

Ok, I'll go, I hope I sink out, thus allowing me the freedom of putting a gun in my mouth. Entering a thermal with twenty other pilots, my usually aggressive climbing style dashed, my new style an apology, "Excuse me, I'll just be floating around over here, you assholes just go ahead, climb on through." Gangreen is flying poorly, bouncing roughly along the course, as if putting golf balls down a gravel road. We suck. The Ruskis move ahead of us on the first day. Gangreen, frustrated and tired, frustrated at being out-partied, a rare thing indeed, but being out flown by guys who we helped get new gliders, we want those gliders back. With no relief for us in sight, Gangreen needs a plan, needs to regroup, our dragging asses ready to quit, our fearless leader, CG, rallying, coming up with a plan, yeah, a plan, yeah. CG's plan is likened to a plane crash, formed around one sentence, "I don't think they have tequila in Russia."

Yeah, tequila, we will thrash them with tequila and dancing, yeah, dancing in a smoke-filled bar, yeah; we'll beat those Russians at our own game, even if it kills us.

After dinner, with Gangreen revitalized and refreshed, our nasty hangovers gone, our leader implements a plan of action, ambushing the Ruskis by luring them into the van, taking the party on the road to a local biker bar.

We arrive at the biker bar, its locals straightforward Americans, keeping the Dunlap tattoo artists in business, the matching bikers, dressed in dark, each biker a Hell's Angel wanna-be, each biker wearing leather chaps, in the back pocket of these chaps, hiding but not hiding, large bulging wallets, the wallets attached to gaudy metal chains, the chains entering their chaps through the zippers, where possibly they are bolted to their balls. Wild haired biker babes, squatting on barstools, scowl at our entry, the women's attire, missing teeth and face wrinkles, their wrinkles not unlike tattoos, resembling the grand canyon, the bar's ambiance blaring, "Crystal meth sold here."

Fifteen of us enter the zoo, safety in numbers, our herd against theirs, sticking together, hoping not to be singled out for a quick mugging in the little boy's room. Smelly is the bar and rough is the establishment, we obviously do not fit in, this place is where we may be injured, where we may bleed, where the bathroom is off-limits, this place is perfect for our plans.

CG orders tequila all around, page one of the blueprints set into motion, the Russians unaware, the plan working smoothly. Squaring off at a table, Gangreen shows the Russians how to properly drink tequila: lick the salt from your hand, shoot the shot and then suck back the lime, lick the salt, shoot the shot, suck back the lime; after five shots each, the Russians begin to get the hang of it. The Russians, being Russians, of course want vodka, but the tequila is free and the Russians are poor, and CG is plying them with all the free tequila they want. We know better than to feed Dogz tequila in a public place, our experience being that the liquid is known to short-circuit the half-breed's DNA. The sight of Dogz keeping pace, shot for shot, with the Russians looks to be the possible weak link in our plan. A plan that, too soon, is going to blow in ways we don't even see coming.

Long hair, hard rock, the loud band starts, the Russians, good dancers and finding their rhythm, the dance floor filling with patrons and a party is under way. After midnight, the bar packed, dance floor a-rocking, sweating dancer biker booty bouncing off sweating pilot booty, the over-exuberant Russians choose to heighten the dancing frenzy by assembling chicken fights on the dance floor, one of the Ruskis climbing up on Krown's back, with the other two Russians forming another human tower.

Fun drunken buffoonery is what it is, and it is not lasting long, as Krown is drunk and the Russian is drunk and Krown loses his balance, stumbling sideways into the stage, causing the upper half of the tower to come toppling over, depositing the heavy Russian into the singer's microphone.

The singer immediately quits singing because he is falling backwards into the drum set, the drum set quits drumming as it is forced backwards into the drummer, the drummer quits sitting as he is falling off the back of the stage. The new rhythms in the bar, crash, boom, bang, the sounds of wreckage, followed by the ringing of fallen cymbals, their hum fading into mounting silence.

Bikers flanking left of us, bikers flanking right, bikers on our frontlines, we are surrounded, an easy escape not forthcoming, conflict in the air, the cause and effect of the failed chicken fight, like that of the black and white turd discharged on the picnic bench, not good. We look at the bikers and they look at us, we look between them for the nearest exit and they look at us like rotten meat.

The ugly bar owner, with three teeth in her head, breaks the silence, her eyes beaming at CG, since he is sitting at the bar right in front of her, yelling at the top of her lungs, "Get those fuckers out of here!"

CG replies back, "Get the fuckers out yourself, you fucking ugly old hag."

She, ready to blow like a volcano, looks at the bouncer, who is also big and ugly, his mouth showing the same lack of basic dental hygiene. The ugly old hag (possibly the bouncer's mom?) points at CG and screeches, "Throw this asshole out of here first!"

'Tis now the fight starts, singer versus Russian, pushing and shoving, followed by bikers versus pilots, fists flying, drinks spilling, tables knocked over, the rotting meat who just wrecked the stage scrambling for the exits. The bouncer is truly the biggest man in the room, weighing 250 pounds with overlapping tattoos, who probably has not showered since working on his Harley, pumping iron in front of his TV with earrings like whore hoops, the bouncer crosses the room, heading for CG, prepared to carry out the old hag's orders, Dogz crossing the room, heading for the bouncer, CG trying to fight his way towards the front door, Dogz struggling through the bar room bodies, trying to defend his friend CG, the bouncer closing in on CG and, from his boot, pulling out a knife with six inches of blade, CG unaware of the bouncer coming for his back, Dogz seeing the bouncer lifting the knife, readying it for the strike, its blade reflecting in the neon lights, only seconds from it plunging into CG's back.

Dogz, crazed like an Indian warrior, hell bent on saving his chief, gallops through the white men, leaps and grabs the bouncer by the hair with both hands, and yanks the 250-pound man backwards off his feet.

The bouncer is pulled backwards, incapacitated, his heels dragging across the dirty wooden floor, his body weight hanging from his hair, his long biker hair held tightly by Dogz, the bouncer's polished six-inch blade still in his hand, available for inflicting pain.

In his futile attempt to regain his footing, the bouncer struggles to free his hair from Dogz's grip, violently shaking his head, but the bouncer's hair, suspended by his 250 pounds, rips right out of his scalp, setting the bouncer free from his hair, the force of gravity not treating the bouncer well, crashing his hair-stripped head to the ground. Einstein, the bouncer, bounces his own head on the bar room floor, losing his grip on the knife and knocking himself unconscious.

In the ensuing chaos, CG grabs the fallen weapon and scuffles quickly across the bar room floor, joining the conga line formed by Dogz, with both his fists full of hair, and the other pilots high-stepping their way out the front door.

"Head for the van!" CG yells.

"I got my scalp!" yells Dogz in reply.

Enter parking lot, stage right, running for our lives. Hang gliders still tied to the roof of our vehicle.

Eight sweaty drunks pile into one 6-person Astro van, private parts scrunched, armpits in faces, blood on the upholstery and CG, for once, admittedly too drunk to drive. Greg, the most sober of us, jumps in and takes over as driver, his foot working the accelerator as we attempt our daring escape through the parking lot. In the back seat, Dogz shakes his fists full of hair, forcing the occupants of the van to behold his new conquests.

"Look!" he yells, "I got my scalp! Hey, look! I got my scalp!"

The Russians can't understand him, and the rest of us Americans couldn't care less. But Dogz, the half-breed, riding high on tequila, wild and free, his eyes insane, rapture in his voice, continues to crow at the top of his lungs, "I got my scalp! I got my scalp!"

To Dogz's mind, this scalping is his rite of passage, his symbol of entering manhood, and he is not gaining the recognition from his tribe that he feels he deserves. His great deed is going ignored, his ego insufficiently stroked, his greatness unrewarded. Dogz loses his mind.

"Punch it!" he yells, and dives forward from the back seat, his hands full of scalp, to push down on the driver's foot, moving the accelerator pedal forward.

The vehicle shoots across the parking lot, taking the driver by surprise. Greg, caught off guard, quickly yanks the steering wheel to the right, causing the vehicle to slide sideways, the moving projectile now fishtailing across the gravel, its rear bumper just missing the long line of parked motorcycles, the vehicle's jerky motions creating contact between the occupants' skulls. Dogz, still unrestrained, keeps pressing the accelerator. Tires spit gravel; bikers stand outside to flip us off, when our spinning tires finally develop enough traction to lurch us into the night.

I struggle to get my hands leashed around Dogz, while CG tries to pull him from the front seat. Dogz fights us like a rabid coyote, his strength overwhelming, his war cries still penetrating the van.

"I got my scalp!"

Dogz's man spirit has left his body, replaced by a rabid coyote spirit, his soul's metamorphosis triggered possibly by his first scalping, or by his warrior spirit set free in the knife fight, or possibly by the tequila. No matter, the trigger is pulled, and it is causing a great deal of anguish, with possible destruction and maybe police intervention and pain as a side effect.

I jerk Dogz's hair as hard as I can, and still he pushes the gas. CG punches him in the back of the head and then chokes him around the neck, and still he pushes the gas. Greg fights the speeding van by stomping down on the brake pedal, thus keeping the van under control but heating up the brakes. The Russians, catching a whiff of burning disaster on the horizon, jump in, pulling on Dogz's legs. With CG beating on his arm and me pulling his hair, Dogz finally releases the gas pedal and sits up in his seat, slowing down the van, but not his war cries.

"I got my scalp! Look, I got my scalp!"

"Fuck the hair, Dogz," I say. I am sick of his screaming and just want to relax. We all just want to relax, but that is not to be. The rabid coyote spirit has us under its spell, its voodoo lulling us into a false sense of security, and we let Dogz go. Our mistake. Dogz is biding his time, watching for a weakness before striking again.

Dogz suddenly forces himself past his handlers and dives under the driver's-side dashboard, pounding the gas pedal with his scalp-filled hands, a fresh round of war cries piercing like arrows. This time he is not going to let up.

The speeding vehicle, just rounding a corner, shoots across the road, and then leaves the road, climbing up a hill on an angle. I watch the whole thing unfold. It's like watching the dentist's long needle squirt fluid out its end, just before your pain.

Greg reacts quickly at the wheel, both feet slamming the brake pedal to the floor. He does a fine job of getting the van stopped, but it is too late: the top-heavy weight of the gliders on the roof pulls us over, the passenger side slams the pavement. The van hits hard, landing back in the road, passenger-side down, producing a vicious crash that sounds eerily like a drum set falling from a stage. People inside monkey-pile on top of each other, the sweaty human bodies stuck together like chunks of wet cotton.

Inside the van, anarchy reigns.

"Kill him! Let's kill Dogz! Which body is his? Kill him!"

As usual, Dogz has lucked out, landing on top of the monkey pile. Hearing that his life is about to be cut short, he attempts to escape by kicking at the wind shield with the heel of his boot, but is unable to break it after the third try. Inside the toppled van, we try to get ahold of Dogz, possibly for an inquisition, maybe to hang him, maybe to break his bones slowly, maybe to send him back to the bar alone. As we talked of torture, Dogz pulls the handle on the driver's side door, now the top of the van, forcing it up, and climbs out. The madman, drunk with freedom, runs into the dark of the woods, still yelling like a wild Indian.

"I got my scalp!"

The Russians, squashed in the van about mid-pile, are learning first-hand some seriously ugly American hospitality. We slowly untangle ourselves and climb out of the wreck, still drunk, two miles from camp at two in the morning, with no working auto, and nursing numerous cuts and bruises. We are sure of only two things: we have a long walk back to camp, and Dogz is dead meat.

Six of us struggle down the road back to camp, bent on revenge, leaving CG prone in a ditch next to his overturned van, bleeding and sleeping, yet unfazed, having received a wild punch to his forehead. Some of us discuss revenge in Russian, some of us carry clubs from the forest, all of us hope to catch Dogz unawares.

CG is later awakened by a passer-by who, seeing the over-turned van and the unmoving body beside it, shouts, "I think he's dead!" CG startles the girl by opening his blood-covered eyes and spinning his unbelievable yarn. Before long, the band members from the bar pull over in their bus to inspect the wreck, too, and CG finds himself explaining how sorry he is. CG somehow con-vinces the twenty strangers aboard the band's bus to help him roll the van upright, and they succeed in rotating the van back onto its wheels. Unfortunately, its transmission is stuck in neutral and gaining speed downhill, without a driver, causing CG to chase it down on foot. It's no use. He watches in horror as his runaway van crashes into the front of the band's bus. He counts out hun-dred dollar bills as fast as he can, shoveling them into the singer's hand, hoping the money will save him from getting a beating by the band.

Dogz, meanwhile, has escaped back to camp, where I find him rooting around in the dark Gangreen trailer for various pyro-technic hazards. I explain that he is being an asshole and that peo-ple want to kill him. Heedless, Dogz proceeds to loudly detonate several large explosives, lighting up the campground while shout-ing, "I got my scalp!" Fifty pissed-off pilots awake to the sound of Dogz's explosions at three in the morning, and when Dogz finally hits the wall and is snoring in bed, CG is loading his pistol, gun-ning for him.

My gut tells me he's coming, and I know his rage may well be uncontrollable. Exhausted but not sleeping, sensing the danger, I lie wide awake at the other end of the Gangreen trailer, making sure I stay awake as Dogs snores like a broken tuba. CG pulls the van up to the trailer. He is now a rabid grizzly bear coming to con-front an inert rabid coyote. He bursts out of the van, its engine still running, its lights pointed at the entry, holding his gun in one hand,

and yanks open the Gangreen trailer door with the other. CG yells for Dogz and Dogz keeps on snoring; CG stomps down the hallway like Godzilla and Dogz keeps on snoring; CG kicks open Dogz's bedroom door and Dogz keeps on snoring; CG points the pistol at the Coyote's unmoving body and Dogz keeps on snoring.

"He saved your life tonight!" I shout from the security of my bedroom, and Dogz keeps on snoring. CG realizes through his anger that Dogz did save his life tonight. He uncocks his firearm and goes home, and Dogz keeps on snoring.

At the pilots meeting the next morning, after the chicken fights, bar fights, the knife fight, the scalping, the van demolition, crashing into the band's bus, the explosives, and the gun play – did I miss anything? – Gangreen's name is rotten meat. We try to hide our red eyes, like a California State Trooper behind green mirrored sun glasses, with our hangovers exploding like Mt. Saint Helens, the debris from the volcanic blast parked on launch, its passenger-side mirror crushed into the door panel, the windows scarred, their one clear surface covered with large star-like patterns, and Krown's demo gliders still tied to the racks, unscathed. On the van's floor, broken glass, Russian footprints, biker hair, pilot blood, a dangerous knife and one empty tequila bottle. Other than the competition task call, the meet director, like a Baptist preacher, dedicates the entire meeting to lecturing about irresponsible, grown adults acting like spoiled children, their actions setting a bad example for visiting dignitaries from a foreign country. But Gangreen doesn't really care, because our goal was to entertain the Russians, American Wild West style, and that we have done quite well.

CHAPTER NINE

Gary

My mind does not creep around the concept of life and death. I am unable to change my past, good or bad; I just live life, hoping my death is fast and honorable. But if I could change a story this is the one. The story about to unfold is about what happens in life because of death, and I have had the fortune, or misfortune, of experiencing a soul-changing amount of instant loss.

My friend Gary was a good, unselfish man, kind of crew cut, maybe a military son, his past I know not, his legs swinging in easy step, his free-flowing arms creating his walk, his walk expressing a man happy in his own skin, his path leading to his favorite subjects, laughing and giving. Laughing was his game, and the more, the better. Hang Gliding or loving brought him his greatest smiles, his life driven by a burning desire to make others smile with him. He loved for people to experience the sky, to learn to fly, side by side with him, tandem hang gliding. His free and easy smile was a gift he was born with and his legacy to our world. Gary's ability to put his tandem passengers at ease was exceptional. He could meet a stranger on the street and explain through his smile about hang gliding, and in pointed conversation find that particular person's dreams of flying and convince them to fulfill their dreams and fly with him. He would sell people on their dreams of flight like a preacher sells a follower on heaven. Maybe when Gary died, he was called up to the spirit world to help teach the newest angels how to use their wings.

During the years of my travels to some of the best flying sites in the country, I often bumped into Gary. We bonded instantly. I think he got along with everybody. Every time we saw each other, it was as if no time had passed. We would fly and camp together, sharing meals over a fire and swapping stories with other travelers who sprout wings. The day he died, Gary and I played with our lunches, flirted with the clean-cut waitress, knowing she would never sleep with either of us unshaven, stinky, camping-in-our-trucks, wild-haired hang addicts. We laughed at ourselves, sharing our lives together in Telluride, Colorado. All along Telluride's boardwalk, we two fast-talking wing nuts interviewed tourists and locals in our search for any living soul with a brain and possibly a driver's license, a beautiful girl would be nice, to bring our retrieval truck from launch up in the alpine tundra down the steep four-wheel-drive road to the grassy cow pasture in the LZ to pick us up when we finished the day's flight. When the aforementioned truck, its lumber rack filled with gliders, the bed filled with pilots, pulled to the curb on Main Street, and the driver asked us if we'd scored a victim yet to drive the truck back down the mountain, our response was negative. Because every person in the truck planned to fly and we found no driver, we were stuck leaving it parked on top.

Screw it, it's time to head to launch, let's go.

With no further prompting needed, we squeeze our bodies into the overfilled truck and head up the hill. Ten pilots and no retrieval driver fill the official Telluride Air Force Club truck, a beat-up $1,000 blue Dodge pick-up, full of dents and rust, its bald tires climbing the steep, rough, boulder-filled, potholed, rocky, dusty road. The truck slips and slides, spinning its tires through a procession of switchbacks, cutting through golden and green aspen forests, slipping under ski lifts, rumbling between large granite spires, and then diving into deep, cool mosquito-swarming pine forests. I bounce along in the back, encircled by the extended arms of the immeasurable San Juan Mountains, feeling as if I am being allowed a quick visit into this amphitheater of the gods. We park the truck on top of the world. Below us, a bouncy blue river, centered in the civilized valley, long fingers of deep green forest climbing sharply from the valley floor, encircling islands of red crumbling cliffs, down past it all, brown and golden brush strokes draining from the high yellow and purple basins, the basins adjoining the long black saw-tooth granite ridges, which end, volcanically, in sheens of reflective black rock piles that look like pools of frozen tears spilled by the lonely black buttresses, their stoic crowns piercing the sapphire blue skies.

We hang glider junkies assemble our wings on a grassy ridge affectionately called Gold Hill Launch. Covered in snow most of the year, with thick green grass growing here during the short Colorado summer, today it is shining in the sun, carpeted in the golden dying grasses that are characteristic of autumn.

Gary and I launch apart and meet in the middle, flying tip-to-tip together, carving our gliders like skis in powdered snow, around and around, gaining in the thermals, diving into wind gusts, racing through the sink, our bodies swinging left and right, forward and back, shifting our weight in a dance, controlling our direction of travel, searching for another thermal and latching onto it, following the thermal as if following a puff of steam on its journey to the clouds.

A couple of hours of unadulterated heaven on earth are followed by the hazy red sun setting over the distant mountain ranges. With dusk approaching, I tear myself from the heights, heeding to caution, and head downward for a landing next to the town of Telluride. Oops Landing Area is where we planned to land and it is a big field, randomly speckled with leg-breaking gopher holes and welcoming patches of soft marsh grass. Approaching in an aircraft through the thin air of 9,000 feet into this landing zone makes setting down exactly where you planned improbable at best. After making safe contact with the earth, I proceed to break down my glider, knowing that Gary is not far behind me.

A soft, slight breeze ruffles my sail, the familiar, comforting sound suddenly disrupted by a loud snap, the sound bringing instant repulsion to my mind. I know that sound, the sound of a hang glider breaking in two. I know that hang gliding is dangerous and love is dangerous and that I have seen more death and disaster, love and loss in my life than I care to hold in my heart, but the sound of Gary's glider breaking apart sets in motion the end of his life and the start of my heart being completely torn apart and then completely rebuilt in the next two days of my life. I can feel my heart race with sickening adrenaline, my body goes rigid, my hands squeeze into fists; in my ears, I hear my voice scream, Oh, my god, Gary, throw your chute, throw your chute, throw your chute... With my heart in my throat, I look up.

Gary, so in love with the sky, hoping this day would never end, followed a spectacular flight with a grand finale: he began performing aerobatic stunts, pushing the limits of his uncertified prototype hang glider at 1,500 feet over the Telluride valley floor. Rumor has it that he was told not to do aerobatics with it, but we will never know, will we?

Oh, my god, help him. Gary is pinned flat against the sail, its nose pointed at the ground, his head pointed at the sky, his body aligned with the sail and facing away from the center of the spin, the whole disaster falling rapidly, as if a flattened badminton birdie rotating around the nose. One full revolution occurs as he descends to 800 feet, another half-revolution and I can see him looking at his arms, unable to get them free, his struggle in vain, the G forces squeezing him helplessly against the sail. Each time the

glider comes around, he loses another 300 feet. I can get a look at
Gary for no more than half of the spin, his helmet thrashing loosely
around the stationary body. Three times he spins his arms, moving
at the elbows, but his shoulders are pinned by wreckage and inertia, and each time he comes around, his predicament doesn't
change. Between the G forces holding his arms in place and the
metal that once was the control frame entangling him, he is unable
to throw his life-saving parachute. Gary hits the ground so hard
that he bounces back up and then hits it again. I've carried that
memory, hidden in my heart, until this very sentence, where now
maybe I can set it – and myself – free. I hope somewhere he is
reading this and remembers me, too.

He hits the ground 100 yards across the field from where I'm
standing. Right next to his wreckage stands a large dead pine tree.
I remember that dead tree. I remember running for him, my mind
wondering how anyone can live through that fall to earth. When I
reach him, he is lying on his back, his eyes are open and he is staring into the sky, his glider lying crumpled in a pile behind him. I
stand over him, looking into his eyes, and think maybe he is ok and
he is going to sit up and say something like, "Dude, did you see
that?" But, kneeling down and touching him, I know he is already
dead. I feel his neck for a pulse, gone. I feel his mouth for breath,
gone. I yell into my radio for the other pilots, who have landed in
the town park, to call 911.

"Emergency in Oops Field," I say, then go to work. Whisked
into rescue mode, I attempt to bring him back to life with CPR.
Tears run down my face as I pump his lifeless chest with my
hands, put my lips to his mouth and share my breathing, counting
out the sequence, breath one and two, chest compressions, one,
two, three, four, five, and breathe, one and two and… time after
time, I rotate between both. Five minutes into my attempts to

bring Gary back to life, his body performs its final action, vomiting his lunch onto my skin. I crack, unable to control my emotions. I lose control, I lose count of breaths to pumps, tears, puke, anger, sorrow as I am giving up hope, the ambulance crew shows up, taking over.

People and the pilots who landed after us begin gathering at the impact zone. While I finish breaking down my glider, many try to comfort me, but no words or emotions will I let penetrate the shield I have just implanted around my heart. Leaving Oops Field, I march alone, through the ugly green grass full of fucking gopher holes, back to that goddamned town. I won't talk to anyone, shunning any help from the people who love me. I detest them all. Fuck you, I say, stay away from me. God, I'm an asshole.

That's it, I think, I'm going to quit hang gliding and begin a nice, normal life, stuck to the ground. I lie on my bed in the back of my van, drinking alone, absorbing Olympia beer (Gary's most shared beverage), mentally beating myself up, my train of thought going something like, I didn't save him, what went wrong, god life sucks, I am out of here tomorrow. Each gulp I inject tastes of anger. I stare into the darkness, my mind slowly dulling until I finally pass out.

I sleep until the following dawn, when I am awakened by a pounding on my van. It is Mad Mitch, a man some say was raised by wolves, don't you know. He must have been elected by our fellow friends to give me a brother-to-brother pep talk, but I won't let his words penetrate the maze in my head or the safeguard around my heart. I try to get Mitch to leave me alone, but you don't tell Mitch, he tells you. He says it like it is, "You will get over it," and that if I puss out and quit hang gliding I will dishonor Gary's memory or some shit like that. I say fuck it, go away, and, ridding myself of him, I start up the van and limp her out of town.

I am escaping from Telluride, leaving the world of hang gliding, the world I love, leaving it forever, on the starting day of the
Telluride Hang Gliding Festival. I don't care. Shedding tears,
beating myself up, running away, changing my life, I am not seeing anything. My van moves me down that ugly San Juan Valley.
The oncoming traffic is becoming jeopardized by my lack of attention, so at Placerville I abandon the pavement and begin traveling a
less populated, snaky dirt road, climbing through another repulsive
canyon, working my way back home. Motivating the van slowly
up the narrow canyon, I leave lots of time for feeling sorry for myself, when this black crow flies into my space and begins soaring
back and forth in front of the moving van. It takes it a little while,
but eventually the crow gets my attention. The black crow is a
freak, because it grows in its collection of black feathers one white
feather. The freaky bird keeps flying back and forth in front of me,
seems to be maintaining pace with the van, not but ten yards ahead
of me, occasionally turning its head and looking back, as if gauging a correct distance between us, we travel up the canyon together. It stays with me for what must be only a minute, but during
that time, I begin feeling affected by it, as if the crow is trying to
tell me something, feeling it is somehow transmitting to me, communicating without words, possibly a contact from the spirit world,
saying, "Do what you love and set yourself free. Gary is going to
be ok." My vehicle comes to a stop, the crow flies away, and, unprepared, my heart bursts open and my tears pour out, and there I
sit, sobbing.

I'm not sure how long I sit there, but slowly my body stops
shaking, my eyes running out of tears, my soul completely cleaning itself out, the crack in my heart free to mend, entering the void,
a feeling of peace, I am on the road to recovery. I understand now

what needs to be done. With Mitch's words in my head ringing true, I turn the van around, striking the highway back to Telluride.

CHAPTER TEN

Telluride

In September, the hang gliding world converges on the town of Telluride, Colorado for the Telluride Hang Gliding Festival. Telluride boasts the most astonishing topography for flying in the USA. Its inhabitants, surrounded by rugged mountains, accentuated by steep climaxing walls and plunging canyons, hide their treasures of gold and silver; plunging waterfalls spray mist into deep fragmented chasms, the chasm bottoms filled with beaver ponds, rivers, creeks, forests, and willow thickets. The abundant plant life, embraced by the tall walls of dark granite, anticipates a short burst of photosynthesis with a visit from the passing sun, the high elevation's temperatures swinging from cold finger mornings to sunburnt afternoons.

Concealed within one of these Rocky Mountain canyons, a place once home to glaciers and gun fights, sits the town of Telluride, named by the early pioneers. It was a name given by the early settlers – law abiding citizens who fled the lawless mining town, on horseback escaping from the heavy drinking, gun happy, gambling, whoring, wild mountain men, the escapees shouting an intimidating warning, turned catchy slogan, to those heading high up into the mountains: "To Hell you ride!" That's Telluride.

The town of Telluride nowadays is built around children and family, fun and adventure, sin and debauchery, Sodom and Gomorra, money and death. It is a mansion to some of Hollywood's rich, and a shack to the happily poor and stoned ski bums; it is a dark, struggling cave to men making a meager living in old mining shafts, and an income-producing apartment to bar maids slinging drinks; and it is an adventure playground to the greatest hang gliding festival on earth. With its reputation for wild nights and wild days in the wild west, the festival's proven standing of non-stop fun pulls pilots in from around the universe, including the elite of the elite. The elite flying humans, amazing wing nuts of the anti-gravity, structurally stable, mentally questionable, loop-de-loop flying brother- and sisterhood, otherwise known as aerobatic pilots.

(Mitch McAleer going upside down over Telluride)

Aerobatic pilots are strange creatures who have a mastery over gravity immortal, maybe gaining their skills training like bats, sleeping upside down, navigating the sky with weird sonar that always finds the right side up. Possibly their neck biting, blood sucking night time activities continue to keep them alive for one more round of aerobatic, blood curdling fervor. These superhumans, who were possibly birds in a previous life, push the limits of their wings so far beyond what mortals can understand that the untrained, when watching from a safe distance, cannot discern if the wing is right side up or right side down. Spectators watching in awe wonder where is the right wing or the left wing, the gliders swooping end over end, side beyond side. Barrel rolling spins, stalls, wing walks, tail slides, butt puckers… all of the maneuvers streaming red parallel indicator smoke from their wing tips, the pilots as if artists doodling on a blue sky tablet with matching red streaks of paint. Or blood, as the case may sometimes sadly be, as it was with my friend Gary, who got a job with the angels in heaven just not two days before. Following my intense breakdown in the canyon, prompted by the freaky crow, I ultimately returned to Telluride and the comforting arms of my friends. I was still shaken up, but willing to strap my wings back on and also get the opportunity to watch the best of the best preform in the skies over Telluride.

Center stage for the festival is the Telluride town park, and landing a hang glider in the park is like landing a jet on an aircraft carrier, but your jet is without engines, meaning every decision used, from approach to touchdown, better be perfect, because you get no second chance. The dangerously small, rectangular field, where the ego-boosting throngs come to watch the landings, like waiting for a wreck at a NASCAR race, is surrounded by 60' tall wing-grabbing cottonwood trees, high voltage power lines strung tightly across its approach pattern, and solid, immoveable objects protruding from everywhere into the final approach route: a parking lot covered in cars, buildings, and skin-tearing baseball backstops. Landing there devoid of angst is a long shot at best.

Spectators watch the show from below, necks tilted back except for those of the children lying in the grass, all eyes skyward as, thousands of feet over the valley floor, the festival's first pilot enters the aerobatic envelope and starts his routine. The athlete points the nose of his glider vertically down, its momentum falling through the sky, searching for 80 mph, reaching full speed, the sounds emanating from his tortured wing like that of a screaming jet, minus the engine, the hurtling glider carving through the bottom arc of the circle and, pitching vertically against gravity, straight back up from where he came. Rising, through the top arc of the circle carving upside down, releasing energy from the wing as it deliberately goes completely inverted, the screaming wing sound goes eerily quiet as the pilot's body swoops over the top, his feelings – of elation or terror – all hidden by his sail from the spectators below. And then again the pilot hooks up with gravity like a lightning bolt, diving straight for the ground, his imaginary jet engine igniting its energy, vibrating and electrifying the air.

We grounded mortals, who call insanity by name, witness the gliders leaping overhead, their manipulation of flight leaving us breathless, our hearts rushed into a gag, our hands, squeezed into fists, settling on folded arms, our body language an involuntary catering to awe. There is not a sound in the crowd, except for the announcer, who screams words of encouragement and flagrant reverence for the blaring wing performing in the sky, the best pilots that mankind has to offer and that God can taketh away.

During the weeklong festival, when not watching the aerobatics perform, the rest of us mortals fly around in these spectacular mountains, punching through clouds, sucking supplemental oxygen, soaring from peak to peak, cloud to cloud, climbing to the incredible altitude of 22,700 feet, a height that makes the San Juan Mountains, spread out far below, look like hills. As for me, my recent brush with Gary's death had put the fear of God in me; I obeyed the laws, never flying above 18,000 feet during my exciting three hour lap around the mountains, my fingers freezing, my oxygen-starved brain returning back to earth, coming in to land in the Telluride town park and gliding across the field... and then slamming the nose of my wing into the ground while trying to land in the thin air at 9,000 feet, the crowd watching yelling at me in unison, "WACK!" My ego-crushing crash ends up costing me another 75 bucks by safely snapping a piece of designed-to-break aluminum tubing. I remove my helmet from my head, my oxygen from my nose, peel off my stinky, snotty Neoprene face cover, and acknowledge the cheering crowd with an upside-down frown locked on my face from ear to ear. I am happy just to be here. Soaring in the heavens or living on the earth, Telluride is 100 % emotion.

Do you want me to tell you a secret? If you're sitting on a barstool in a Telluride meat market when the hounds are out and the playing field is wide open, and you commence to plug one nostril and sniff loudly, repeating the function on the other side, this act will incite the local mating call, and once the evening's mate is found and the act is consummated and then you finally run out of cocaine, you won't lose your girlfriend, you'll just lose your turn, as she goes off in search of more fertile hunting ground.

On the first night of the festival, JT uses this mating call to hook up with a mate. Known only as The Wild Thing, her beauty is fading fast, her spirit intense, her eyes never looking at me, never stopping, always moving, blinking, rolling around, her dedicated mind constantly looking for her next snort. JT is a wild child in his own right, his eyes always red, their gaze wide and alert, their energy beaming a restless genius, his brain holding every fact ever passed by it, a constant intake of THC helping keep his genius relaxed, his longing for wild things keeping ahold of her as long as she didn't bite. His problems begin when he finally consummates the deed and the bars are closed and he gets tired of her, and he still possesses cocaine but The Wild Thing is not done with JT.

At around two in the morning, after closing down the bars, I stumble along the dark sidewalk to the Telluride town park and pass out alone in my van. Not for long, however, for JT slithers across town about an hour later, following a round-about hiking path through the forest in a desperate attempt to escape from his female Wild Thing, who is just getting warmed up. JT finds my van, and, thereby rousting me from a sound sleep, looks to me for a hiding place. The only place I can think of at the moment is underneath the van.

JT is riding on desperation and amazes me by taking up my offer. It is a rainy night and the van is leaking oil, but JT is frantic to escape and willing to confront anything but The Wild Thing. He wraps himself up like a cocoon in a sleeping bag and tarp, stuffs himself under the van and falls asleep.

Round about four AM, The Wild Thing tracks her prey through the forest, her survival instincts uncanny, and beats her paw on the paint of my van.

"Where is JT?" she howls. "Get up, where is JT?"

I open my window just wide enough to say, "Hey, bitch, I haven't seen him, so go away." Oh, what was JT thinking? The Wild Thing is uglier in the dark than the light. If he would have just lain still, everything would have been fine, but, no, JT's fatal mistake is to move inside the tarp, the plastic crinkling sound giving him away. Her bunny rabbit hearing picks up his rustling, JT's crinkly tarp resonating into the still night, its effect like ping pong balls bouncing in a marble hall, the all-inclusive noise coming from under my vehicle, below her knees, alerting the ugly but wise Wild Thing to his hiding place. Un-snookered, she looks under the van, catching me lying and finding JT's former hiding place. Oh, that damned tarp. She wiggles under the van, trying to attach herself to JT, like a sucker fish attaches to a shark.

JT sleeps naked, I soon learn. In his escape from her clutches, he proceeds to roll out from under the far side of the van, getting leaves and gravel stuck to his nakedness. Then he scampers off like a squirrel, no shoes, no shirt, no pants, no service, screaming, "Fuck you, bitch!" into the pitch black, drizzling forest.

Rounding five AM, JT finally eludes the cocaine-sniffing Thing for the second time this morning. He straggles back to the van, his naked body washed by the rain, waking me, complaining his way into the comfort of the van, asking me to locate him a towel, my only towel, which rests in my pile of dirty clothes, now dry. JT sleeps, like a coke whore, on the muddy carpet of the 1991 Ford Econoline 250, while I lie in bed, listening to him snore, like Dogz, until nine AM, time to get up, time to go up the hill, time to go hang dangling, tired or not.

The illustriously crazy, but lots of fun Gangreen Hang Gliding Team is set to star next on Telluride's festival roster. Dogz is in the approach pattern for the town park with CG flying the same flight path 200 feet beneath him, when CG notices a small ball of red fire streak in front of his flight path. That irrational Dogz is trying to shoot CG's glider with an emergency signal flare, a ball of burning phosphorous. I'm sure Dogz has his reasons for trying to shoot a flying goose with a roman candle – CG being the unfortunate goose in this case. Needless to say, it is just another one of Dogz's bad ideas.

Streaking past CG's glider, the molten ball of fire shoots like a star into the forest below. What a promiscuous ball of flame it is, too, because it quickly breeds with the dry kindling lying on the forest bed, and rapidly a whole orgy of gnome-like flames is born, fornicating wildly throughout the foliage. Soon the small forest fire has become a big forest fire, and Dogz is in the fire marshal's office begging for mercy. The locals, like the miners from days gone by, want to lynch him from the nearest un-burnt tree. And there, as always, is CG, counting out his pile of hundreds to cover our asses.

Night falls and the fire smokes, crackles and pops on the mountainside above town. The bars on Main Street fill with patrons, eager to watch the dazzling forest fire spread, the most exciting show in town if you don't count the booming liquor business, which is quickly doubling its profits.

Flames leap into the nighttime sky, lighting up town as if it were daylight. Violent orange and blue flames consume tall, tortured trees, their pops and crackles sounding their death songs, their explosions echoing from canyon walls, their pain felt even in the bars on Main Street. Flames march up the hill, cutting a vertical path in favor of nearby multi-million dollar mansions. Twenty-five hard-working volunteer fire fighters have raced from their family dinner tables, called to work by the siren screaming from the roof of the fire station. Forest fire flames reflect off their shiny red fire engines as the firemen raced up Main Street, past the bars full of patrons who cheer on the spinning white lights and welcome sirens. Five fire trucks come to a halt 500 feet below the fire. The well- trained firemen, attempting to squelch the fire, attempting to not get hurt, attempting to keep the fire's price tag low, begin to climb the deep, slippery grass, grunting with sweaty hand-over-hand effort, scaling vertical hillsides with 60-pound packs full of axes and chainsaws and other heavy equipment, climbing onward to go where no fire truck or hose can go.

A hundred acres burn that night, the fire light reflected on the fire chief's office window, an office where Dogz and CG continue peeling In God We Trust hundred dollar bills from their money rolls, placing them softly on the busy fire chief's desk, Dogz looking at arson, CG looking at five grand in cash. After five hours of hard work fighting disaster, a green mountain meadow, its moist grass unable to burn, gives the overwhelmed fire fighters the break they need. The meadow's moisture contains the fire, snuffing out the lively orgy of flames, turning it into measly smoking embers. With the fire now out, partiers and pilots close the overcrowded saloons at two AM and walk out into the wisps of smoke drifting down from the high ridge, the forest fire's lingering odor flowing into town, traveling along Main Street and down into the valley, venting into the desert, as once again, the ashes of Gangreen continue to blow in the wind.

On the day following the fire, one hundred people gather in the Telluride town park to watch another exciting kind of smoke, the thick long streaks of color that stream out of the smoke canisters attached to the gliders entered in the World Aerobatic Championships, the highlight of the Telluride Hang Gliding Festival. On top of Gold Hill launch, the competition pilots wait, patient or excited, all afternoon for the calm late afternoon airflow in which to perform, then, one by one, as their names are called, they dazzle the spectators with their skills.

The large crowd gathered in the Town Park cheers excitedly as the announcer draws their attention to the first competitor, who is now penetrating over the mountains into our view.

His glider glistens in the setting sun, as the crowd watches him maneuver his wing into position and ignite his duel smoke canisters, the two smoking red lines behind the glider highlighting his progress. He begins his routine, the long red streamers of smoke following behind his free-falling glider, his dive straight down, racing with gravity, reaching full speed at 80 miles per hour. Then, turning the tables on himself, he arcs through the bottom of the circle, red streaks rushing back skyward, carving his wing straight away from us, cutting back through his lingering lines of smoke and climbing over the top, the glider going upside down, his body hidden from the passionate feelings of the spectators. An amazing magician, a true competitor, upside down, creating a beautifully executed loop, six more times he loops, thrilling himself and the crowd. His routine finished, four judges tally his score and, to a standing ovation, he times his landing flair perfectly, touching down in the town park with the grace of a swan in front of an amazed humanity, his glider reflecting the glorious sunlight.

Directly overhead, the second competitor enters the aerobatic envelope, preparing himself for the awaiting crowd. Pulling his smoke canister, he begins to dive. Dive, dive, dive, looking down on us, and then his aircraft humps back up to the top, the wing slowing and flopping, not carving over the top, completing his first loop sluggishly, the judges and crowd sensing his mistake, but he makes it. His smoke seems to be flowing slower than the previous competitor's. Dive, dive, dive, he heads earthward again, carrying his speed through the bottom and carving back upward, aiming for the top of another loop, except this time he is too slow and his glider stalls completely upside down, the sun shining on the bottom of his sail, his body hidden above, the whole kit and caboodle parked upside down, the aircraft teetering indecisively across a critical edge of fate. He is now at the mercy of gravity, and it is not kind, for instead of the glider's nose falling forward, the glider's tail decides to be the heavier and it is now slicing through the sky in reverse and backtracking for the earth.

(Gravity takes control)

The unbalanced pilot is experiencing what those unfortunate few call "falling backwards into a disobedient tail slide." Watching this, for me, is like comprehending that a tidal wave is heading for shore. My hair stands up on the back of my balls. Oh, god, please, no more death this week.

For four hundred feet, the pilot's glider slides backwards towards oblivion, wowing the judges with the tail slide, but the pilot, wanting more, pulls another secret trick out of his repertoire, preforming an unplanned maneuver no other competitor has mastered or will attempt, his body falling into the sail and snapping his wing in half. That sound of snapping aluminum echoing from the canyon walls causes my adrenalin to surge like a wave through my body as terror grips spectators in the town park. The ill-fated pilot, as if riding a one wing butterfly, is spinning horizontally attached to his wing, his body revolving on the outside of the spin, the smoke canisters engulfing him in an evil-looking haze.

Oh, the poor man , he spins for the ground, strapped to his glider broken, metal tubing thrashing his torso severely, his body pulled to the outside of the spin in a sadistic game of smoking Crack the Whip. Terror fills the town park, the spectators transfixed, helplessly watching as reality, horror and possible death begin to unfold before their eyes. All at once, voices start yelling up at the hapless pilot, "Throw your chute! Throw your chute!" He must hear us because his chute squirts out from the spinning wreckage.

Oh, great, the people think, he got his chute out. And the chute clears the glider, almost opening; except the spinning wreckage snags the long shroud line connected to the pilot's harness and, in two more full revolutions of the whirling dervish, the unopened chute wraps up like a yo-yo back into his glider. And there the chute flaps in the streaming airflow, snagged on the wing's tip of what used to be a hang glider, its white fabric acting like a plastic bag in the wind. A beyond-repair hang glider and pilot, hooked together, back-to-back, with a very strong strap keeping them bonded, spins madly amidst a plume of red smoke exhausting from the canisters, engulfing the pilot in what looks like a smoldering orange ball, his reserve parachute flapping inside the smoke on the end of his x-wing tip, resembling a flickering red and white flame.

This pilot was obviously a Boy Scout, because he is prepared, carrying on his harness a second emergency parachute, which he now tosses into the atmosphere. Just like the first one, however, the second chute almost opens, but it, too, snags on the thrashing glider and is reeled back unfairly into the wildly spinning and smoking wreckage, its canopy snagging on the opposing end of the wing. Now he is fucked, spinning over the crowd with two flapping rags of what used to be a parachutes streaming on each wing tip, a plume of smoke spewing from his mass of broken wreckage, and the pilot getting tossed around like a rag doll, surviving on what is left of his good karma.

The throng of spectators underneath watches, horrified. Men howl openly. One woman repeats, "Oh my god, oh my god, oh my god," as the helpless pilot's future spins around and around for another 2,000 vertical feet. It isn't until he enters the shade of the valley walls and is 100 feet over the forest of aspen trees, near the edge of the park, that his karma finds him, his swirling, smoking pile of existence magically flopped over, locating him on top of the sail, putting itself between him and the trees, where it floats softly down into the forest, like an angel's feather settling onto the world. The spectators empty out of the park in unison, running into the forest to aid the fellow pilot; a pilot that was not judged today by men holding score cards in the park, but by God.

When we get to him, he is sitting upright, on top of his sail, encircled by the forest, looking as if someone has emptied a red carpenters chalk box over his being, his eyes rolled back in his head, his brain having spun around so radically that he is unable to connect his words, his white parachute, streaked like a tie dyed T shirt, is draped over his lap along with $8,000 worth of destroyed misfortune. Seeing that the dizzy pilot is going to live, the spectators leave the lucky pilot to the professionals and walk back to the park to watch the next competitor try to best that show.

Our next victim flies out over the park, performs two beautiful full-speed loops, his style clean, his speed fast, his routine flawless, and his skills bringing renewed excitement to the overstimulated crowd. Many a yarn was told by the spectators in the bars that night, because the high G forces he creates while carving through the bottom of his third loop, while his aircraft sounds like a screeching chalk board and the mob cheers the man on, breaks his right wing.

Unlike the previous contestant, whose glider sounded like a snap, this glider sounds more like a crushing aluminum can. The broken wing slaps up against the other, still rigid, wing, and one smoke canister released from the glider streaks spastically into the wild blue yonder while his other smoke canister spins round and round, looking like a one-bladed blender, as pieces of aluminum and sailcloth beat together like aluminum chimes with accompanying flapping plastic bags. Broken glider parts depart the wreckage, migrating hither and yon.

Human beings are allowed only so many heart-wrenching experiences before they emotionally crack, and in the town park that day, tears run like egg whites down folks' faces.

A spastic rocket ship, previously a hang glider with a person on board, dropping towards the earth, its occupant soon to become eggshells mixed in a broken omelet of pain.

With a little more harmony than the previous contestant, the relationship between the pilot and his parachute soon became one and he tosses it at the setting San Juan sun. It opens correctly, almost. One piece of the parachute's canopy becomes entangled with the rest, looking from the ground like piece of pie with a large slice missing, the missing canopy section causing his descent rate to accelerate in the thin Colorado air. Five seconds later, the piece of pie that is missing is returned to its rightful place, and the pilot/glider combo decelerates, instantly jolting the glider hard by the full opening of the chute. Gravity elongates the pilot and his glider like a stiff rubber band putting too much G force on the canopy. The overpowered canopy collapses, sending the pilot free-falling for the ground, the glider following in the middle, and the collapsed parachute streaming on top. I close my eyes, unable to hold my gaze, and focus on not crying.

Pop goes the weasel. The sound of the re-inflating parachute canopy bounces me from my stupor. Two collapses later and 500 feet from the valley floor, the pilot, glider and parachute make peace with each other, working correctly together, as they stream, in order, out of the sky, and plow out of sight into the pine forest, next to the red cliffs, below the purple basins, under the eyes of the crying buttress, every single entity gleaming in the last rays of the falling sun.

Cracking tree branches, snapping from the impact of 300 pounds of life and limb, thud sickly as the side of beef slaps its way through the tree tops, impacting the hard, hard ground, following a loud silence. The spectator peace is shattered by the event announcer, yelling, "Do you fuckers on launch hear this radio?

The fucking launch window is closed! There will be no more flying today!"

My nerves are fried. I cannot absorb any more carnage. Only the demon alcohol can wash away the ache, and I turn for the
bars, flowing against the grain of the rescuers streaming for the
abused, my direction opposing all others running for the crash site.
I get ten fucking steps and then my mother's teachings take over,
her words running through my head, "Help others in need." I turn
about face and run with the rest, helping to serve in any way I can.

He is alive, beaten and battered; grinning through an expression of, "Did you see that?" His wrist is possibly broken, leaving
his other hand available for holding the various drinks he is bought
in the bars this evening by his many new fans.

Me? Are you talking to me?

Holy shit, she's a beauty. She just walked off the front page
of Vogue magazine and entered The Last Dollar Saloon, a place
where teeth are the highlight to one's face, and she's talking to me,
and laughing with me – or at me, I am not sure. She only drinks
Cokes, no alcohol; whatever, I figure her husband should be showing up soon. Every swinging dick in the dive is positioning to talk
to me. Ha, I am their conduit to her. I keep acting like myself and
she keeps laughing at my sexist, crude, uncouth, construction
worker potty mouth line of bullshit. A lady in lace and a man with
a cock, what could be better?

Totally floored, are my ears working correctly, you want me
to come to your place for dinner, now? My cock says let's go and
I trail behind it, as if I am her little poodle and she is leading me on
the end of a leash, my tail wagging at my friends as they stand
transfixed, their beers getting warm, watching Beauty and the

Beast cross the bar room floor, with me, myself and I strutting through the exit door.

It isn't dinner, it is seduction, and I am the victim, and what a willing victim I am.

She has me ingesting Ecstasy for desert, a drug designed by Cupid, our clothes are turned into restraints, the toys come out in every color of the rainbow, and just when I think I'm done, she yanks my leash, leading her pet to her bath. Much later, four inches of fluid are left in the bottom of the once-full tub. Not minutes, hours. I feel as if I am in an all-star wrestling match in heaven. A master of orphic animation is she; I am outperformed, ten-fold. Who knows when we slept, if we did, but I know one thing, I never should have set up my wing the following day.

Am I a stud or an idiot? Either way, I am spent, a ecstasy hangover, rug burns, a bath tub spigot gash on my forehead, my pains unresolved by showering. What was her name? What am I doing setting up this aircraft?

What a fool I am.

I get the glider set up correctly because of repetition; it has nothing to do with my brain function. Launch goes well and the first thermal to sixteen grand is delicious. But when I enter the bottom of a cloud over Mt. Sneffels, at 17,000 feet, my brain loses the constant of sight, leaving my eyes nothing to focus on, and my logic redirects itself, my equilibrium becomes unbalanced, my hangover takes over and I become sick. Violently sick, dry heaves sick, sweating body sick, vertigo head spinning sick, a sad state for a sorry marshmallow flying a gram cracker. Barely thinking, my vision blurred, the glider a strange object in my hands, out of body experiences follow up with a running commentary of What am I going to do now, I will never be able to land this thing, help, no one's going to help you, you dumb shit.

A little dot of inert human flesh, way high in the sky, looking like a speck stuck in the great blue, high above the Mt. Sneffels wilderness, the speck experiencing its first panic attack, and that floating speck is sadly me. It is all such a jumble: sweat, panic, altitude sickness, vertigo, at 17,000 feet; flying this hang glider is a mindless soul with no ambition, dropping like a rock. I begin flying flat and level, any slanting to the horizon turning my stomach. I glide for the biggest ranch field I can see, its welcoming green softness ten miles away. A long bumpy glide over the drawn out forests that spill northward from the mountain range and my head continues reeling, I keep looking at the horizon and stop looking down to keep myself from retching again.

Twenty minutes of freezing cold gut wrenching gliding over the sea of trees and then ten more minutes of flying across the scrub oak deltas outside of Ridgeway, Colorado, before I realize my oxygen tank is off. God, how stupid. Turning it on gives me some relief, my plight losing more altitude, gliding back down to nine grand and finally at 500 feet above the ground I drink water without heaving. It is time for me to pick a field, find the wind direction and prepare for my impact.

A soft, green, recently cow-grazed, irrigated pasture serves as the site of my impact. Nothing happens. I have no reactions, I can't rally my fried brain to follow the logical steps needed to perform a landing, so I just fly into the ground, furrowing a divot and generating a splash in the soft wet cow pasture. Cow shit smell is the first realization of any sense entering my addled brain, stinky cow pasture grass on my harness, on my clothes, moist wet fresh stinky cow stench splashed on my face. God, it's good to be back on the ground.

I hitchhike back to Telluride, the glider tied onto the top of the headache rack of a helpful local rancher's pickup truck, my wet cow pasture smell leaving me riding in the bed of the truck, alone. I am fine with that, as it gives me time to beat myself up. How could I have been so stupid, letting my little brain control my life once again?

Back in town, in one stinky piece, I take a quick douche in the frigid river, kind of a self-punishment thing, and head for my cradle in the van before the sun is done.

I awake refreshed, my mistake from the previous day ingrained and forgotten, too embarrassed to let the others in on my foolishness, my excuse to my friends for flying away from the T-town valley include, I enjoyed going cross-country, a little sight-seeing tour, possibly I went looking for my mind.

Today everyone gambles $100 per contestant, puts their ante in the pot, and the first person to land at the Norwood airport 45 miles away wins the pot and takes everyone who lands after them out to dinner and gets to keep the leftover cash. Twenty-five pilots take up the challenge. In the pot is money placed there by many of the best competition pilots from the USA, and winning the money is going to be tough. Today's forecast allows for light wind, so our task is to be into a head wind. Launching and climbing in small gaggles, we travel west, playing leapfrog with each other, circling above and gliding along the sharp ridges covering the north end of the range. Rotating beneath us, sweeping golden, green and red aspen forests, higher up on the mountain's shoulders, deep green pine forests dotted arbitrarily with golden changing September aspens, green meadows follow us up over the ridges, the grasses exposed above tree line turning to golden brown, the mountain peaks gray and black in the baking sun. Flying across the ridge and gaining the other side, the magnificent beauty starts all over again.

Flocks of wings spinning in vertical columns of five and ten hang gliders march along the Northern-most range of the almighty San Juans. Crossing the mountains feverishly as we work our way into the afternoon's increasing headwinds, each thermal tilting us a little more steeply back towards where we were, our columns of lift pushed by the winds in the wrong direction. Upon reaching the plateau and canyon country of the San Miguel river basin, the lift becomes more broken and harder to follow. Each thermal's texture, a strong punch of lift on one half of the circle's circumference and strong sink on the other half. In order to climb in the broken blender, a special soaring technique is incorporated, involving climbing to the top of the lift and coming almost to a complete stop, then falling over the crest of the lift and pulling on the speed, cutting through the sink and once again climbing up to gain elevation, flying as if skateboarders on a ramp, propelling ourselves higher up the sides by thrusting our inertia. Flying away from the mountains into the flats of the mesas, the wind's effects more pronounced, the gaggles of gliders continue slowly traveling forward and over the scrub oak mesas and pine tree canyons of high desert tabletop country of western Colorado.

We work hard at flying in the broken lift, while the headwinds keep us from moving forward efficiently; a few pilots unable to figure out the air's puzzle begin to land on the mesa below. On the edge of the last flat mesa, where its cliffs fall abruptly 1500 feet down to the river, in the bottom of the mile-wide San Miguel river canyon, our forward progress stops, bottling up the 15 competing pilots still in the air like a traffic jam. We are inside the last thermal before the wide canyon crossing, 15 pilots strung out in a long vertical circling column, each competitor peering over the edge of the last big mesa, looking down into the tree-infested canyon, unable to gain the necessary elevation to cross the abyss safe-

ly, the greedy pilots circling on the edge of the precipice, waiting
for a better thermal to show. Our hopes are dashed as the thermal
slowly erodes out from underneath us, leaving us the choice of either landing on top of the mesa or risking our lives crossing the
canyon and continuing on to Norwood. One by one, our country's
best pilots turn away from the canyon crossing, choosing to live
another day over the pot full of cash, and begin landing in the big
flat field on top of the mesa. Determined not to be outdone and to
the astonishment of every competitor, one lone, insane Indian
heads on, gliding into the canyon,. Either his skills are so attuned
with Mother Nature that he sees a secret sign, or he is just crazy,
either way Dogz is choosing the impossible. Those of us still
struggling to stay up in the eroding thermal watch as he leaves the
safety of the final landing area and glides into the shady abyss.
Dogz slices across the canyon opening, his green and white glider
disappearing from the bright sunlight into a backdrop of the ponderosa pine-covered shadows, and the toupee of the steep far-side
canyon walls. He hits not a bump, just as the rest of us had judged,
no thermals thriving in the cool river valley, and Dogz continues to
sink lower and lower. Inside the canyon, where he may bleed,
roars the violent river, its canyon walls include the usual canyon
wall stuff – cliffs, piles of boulders, tall trees, medium trees, small
trees, deep rocky ravines, scrub oak, a snaky two lane road following the river, power lines following the road located under the
power lines, a narrow concrete bridge for crossing the river, and a
small house next to the river, its back yard perhaps the same size as
Dogz's glider. Down and down he sinks into his depression until
300 feet from his demise he hits a little thermal. Oh, he works and
works, round and around, but the son of a bitch thermal fizzles out
like a sparkler on an ice cream cake and now he has to land. Me,
in his predicament, I might pull out my .38 and shoot myself in the

head, getting it over with quickly, but Dogz has other plans. We watch as he follows the river and speeds up his approach for the bridge, throwing in a radical maneuver, he pops up over the power lines, and then back down, gliding like a white water raft along the surface of the river, his wing tips inches from the river's steep embankments, banking his glider up sharply and stalling it into his impact point, the glider falls perfectly centered in the back yard of the residence, stopping his helmet short of a plate glass door. An impossible act, an act never to be repeated, his accomplishment akin to a fighter jet landing undamaged at an airport, on top of the control tower, an inhuman feat by a bird reincarnated as a man, a total miracle has happened at the bottom of Norwood Hill, where no one wins the cash, but even better, Dogz blows the minds of every pilot watching.

The finale of the Telluride hang dog fest is the awards banquet held in the high school gymnasium, with tables, chairs, food, booze, pilots, families, boys and girls. During his first presentation up on stage, the Master of Ceremonies ducks from an attacking bat that has somehow gotten trapped inside the gym and is flying profoundly around the room. The trespassing wild bat dives crazily through the crowd, scaring the children and stirring the mob into a killing frenzy. The bat's icky appearance is denounced by the announcer and riles up the mob to try and catch the thing. When the restless natives climbing on tables and throwing objects fail at catching the bat, they then try killing it. The girls scream, the boys chase it around with brooms, and Gangreen laughs at the antics of this one agile bird-like creature. The bat's black winged mystique sends the humans into frenzy. Eventually, the tired bat is pinned by a broom and the dead carcass sent to his maker, the party moving forward.

Many speakers and many awards, glider paraphernalia given for some special act, others receive cans of Spaghettios – relabeled fish assholes – and a free parachute repack is awarded for anyone having two deployments at once. The Boy Scout aerobat receives an award for throwing two chutes and dutifully on stage repeats the creed, "Be prepared." Another award, the Golden Hammer, goes to the second pilot, who wrecked the most equipment and walked away unhurt. The winner of the prestigious Most Fun on the Ground Award is JT, and the crowd loves it. JT, the mystical character who tamed The Wild Thing, plus a few other willing female participants whose moral fibers could be twisted with his magic dust, is receiving an award. A pornographic trophy made of broken pieces of aluminum glider tubing with rubbers and other sexual paraphernalia glued to it, is to be given to JT, and it is held up on stage for the visiting families to see. It is disgusting, and I love it.

"Speech! Speech!" roars the crowd, many of them knowing JT and knowing to expect the unexpected. He tries to hide under our table, but I point him out to the crowd and as he surfaces he flips me the bird.

JT slowly meanders his way up the aisles, getting slaps on the back by his fellow pilots, many jealous of his legendary sexual exploits, as the Master of Ceremonies expectantly waits up on stage for an extra wild appearance. Not a word leaves JT's mouth as the announcer enlightens the listeners about the mysteries of his deeds, telling pornographic stories in front of the mixed assembly, a few of his sexual partners in attendance, listening uncomfortably, and The Wild Thing perched in the back of the hall like a gargoyle.

"Speech! Speech!"

He is not to leave the stage without a speech. JT raises his arms, waving them up and down, indicating, "Quiet down, people," his actions silencing the room. Two hundred people wait in delight for his words. JT mimics like he has a huge invisible tube in his hand, and bringing it to face level, he shoves the invisible pornographic tube into his open mouth and shows its invisible point by pushing against his opposing cheek with his tongue, his hand sawing the offending item in and out a few times, lowering his hands to his sides, his speech over, the multitudes totally flabbergasted at JT creating an invisible blow job. Laughter races to the surface, uncontrollable, as, in waves, people begin spitting beer and food, and wild animals in the front row throw opened cans of flying fish assholes at JT. JT, using his amazing knack for escaping, jumps ahead of the offending Spaghettios that land on stage. The festival is over and it is a bittersweet ending for me. A festival as untamed and politically incorrect as this happens in one place, and one place only, deep in the mighty San Juans.

(EK @ 22,700' over Telluride)

CHAPTER ELEVEN

The Cauldron of Hell

New Mexico is a land of enchantment, a landscape of beautiful, lonely mountain ranges, hundreds of miles of infinite undisturbed vistas, of many shallow graves, a land where old Mexico crosses into New Mexico and the illegals travel through, becoming New Americans. It's an old and diverse culture where the Spanish rose fell by the wayside and crystal meth became the new state flower, where the county politics are run by the gang bangers, and the retirees hide up near Santa Fe.

Sandia Peak juts like a lone skyscraper out of the flat desert, its penthouse floor overlooking the entire state, the mountain's massive rock walls dividing the high desert of hot southern New Mexico from the sea of cacti and pinions rolling north for cool Colorado. Shear vertical spires generate the mountain; their bases beginning in the climate of the cactus, granite columns then rip up through scrub oak and lodge pole pines, shoved like knives from deep below, the granite knives finishing their climb in the tall cool ponderosa pine forests, 4,000 feet above the valley floor.

Intimidating is what comes to mind when in the company of the mountains. Massive urban sprawl, growing outward from the nucleus of Albuquerque, is stopped by the undeveloped mountain of rock. A 20-person tram is the only way to reach the Sandia Peak from the west side, its thick black cables stretched between tall burnished steel towers, towers that are bolted to the knife rock, each tower advancing 500 feet per step up the contour of the steep rock incline.

New Mexico's Sandia Classic is the most grueling, violent, three-ring flying circus on the competitive flying tour. Its demanding flying conditions lend to pilots with arms strong as a monkeys', brains of a chess player, and the balls from a steel statue of Neptune. A single day's flight tests men's testes on an hourly basis and was, once upon a time, won by a beautiful princess.

To the right of the Sandia launch is a place feared by all, and appropriately named the Cauldron of Hell. This is a place where Mother Nature punches up thermals like NASA punches up rockets. Three monstrous granite buttresses are circumnavigated by an unwieldy granite cliff, the geological combination creating boiling, lifting, roiling invisible air currents that act like Grand Canyon rapids on steroids, turbulent air so violent that it yanks the snot from your hyperventilating face. It's as if riding the rubber ball attached to the ping pong paddle by the rubber band.

Two days before Gangreen arrived at the Classic, a seasoned competition pilot got turned upside down while testing out a new glider prototype over the Cauldron. Tumbling involuntarily, he held tightly onto his controls, avoided falling into the sail, and the glider righted itself, which kept the wing – and the pilot – from breaking.

The previous tumbling is all the talk by the time Gangreen pulls into town in the Mountain King. Other pilots, who heard the tale, become distrustful of their new radically designed glider, causing the manufacturer to be concerned about its stability, so the nervous nanny designer stayed up late in the shop and overnighted to the meet headquarters multiple packages of modified dive recovery systems for all pilots flying said questionable glider.

Meet headquarters is located in a sports bar, and the first evening we arrive in town, Gangreen parks on the bar stools after our long drive, we are given, along with our drinks, packages of parts for said new dive recovery changes. So that night, in the parking lot of the local bar, under the glow of the Mountain King's headlights, we install the new glider parts. Adding new parts to a questionable glider before starting the three-ring death defying circus is making us all nervous nannies, psychologically beating us up, an ominous way of starting seven days of life-threatening adventure.

There is a lot of "over-the-edge" flying at Sandia, but the local girls and boys' hang gliding club tries their best to soften the harsh environment by putting on an excellent deep desert competition, creating a country club atmosphere with luxuries like hotel rooms, hot showers and air conditioning, and riding in comfort to the top of Sandia Peak by means of an aerial tram instead of the back of a dusty truck bouncing up a rough road.

Inside the tram car, pilots and sightseers are magically whisked up the mountain in a nice cool environment, where there is a beautiful view of Albuquerque surrounded by the distant green and red desert. A restaurant and bar on top of Sandia Peak is where the tram, completing its long journey, comes to rest. The danger of mixing hang glider pilots in with the general public is obvious and, too soon, some inquisitive soul starts asking questions. Once people find out that they are going to be watching us run off this mountain in a hang glider, their brains, trained by television, begin asking disrespectful questions of us. They become like six o'clock headline news announcers, telling us about their uncle's cousin's neighbor's friend's belated poodle and cockatoos that were all killed hang gliding, and that hang gliding is for people who are going to die right in front of them and, secretly, they can't wait to see it. Many of the zombies riding the tram hope to be interviewed after the fact by a TV reporter, and then hurry home quickly enough to see themselves on the tube and watch us die re-

peatedly on prime time news. Standard questions I am asked by
these strangers include:

"What happens when the wind stops?"

"Can you control those things?"

"Can you get life insurance?"

"Aren't you scared?"

"Don't your arms get tired from hanging on?" (Like we're
doing chin-ups all day long.)

"Are you married?"

I just feel so threadbare listening to the uninformed that I
usually keep my mouth shut, deferring the answers to others more
patient.

But, on certain occasions when my mouth will not keep quiet, I usually explain that when the wind quits the gliders just fall
out of the sky, all of us hoping we don't get killed, or there is no
control and only half of us will make it through the day, with the
last person left standing winning the trophy. Occasionally, we get
some intelligent questions, like:

"What are they made of?"

"How do you steer?"

"Do you use instruments?"

"How high can you get?"

My answer to that last question is to say I say I got real high
and then I got real high and ended up in heaven circling at 22,700
feet, and they think I'm kidding. I do get a few smiles with that
answer, though.

At the end of the tram cables, in the cool mountain breeze,
high above the Albuquerque smog, the endless desert eroding patterns in the mountain face, we depart the tram and shuffle with the
other tourists along the path, leading past the restaurant, to the
glider set-up area. Trepidation exudes from the set-up area, where

newly modified, untested, faith in the designer, tumbled-only-two-days-earlier hang gliders are being assembled by old friends, doubling as fellow competitors. Many competitors about to be flying the newly modified glider question me, as if I know anything about glider design, their eyes nervous as they ask how I feel about the radical changes to this glider, hoping to find comfort in my words.

In my most educated, serious, experienced, hang glider knowledge buffoonery, I quote my only source on the subject, telling the already skeptical aviator that today is a good day to die. They obviously were hoping for a more technical answer. Instead, they give me a chuckle, a laugh, any sound to mask their anxiety, not sure if I am serious, which is an approach I avoid. Then they give me a look like you're an asshole, and walk away, the pilot wishing to never again ask me anything else, leaving me feeling like the quote I stole from Dogz, who borrowed it from his ancestors, works well for Dogz but not for me. Yes, it is a beautiful day to die.

Thermals begin cooking like boiling pasta up past the tram, powerful wind currents bouncing off the face of the sharp granite spires, rowdily snapping the plastic wind streamers placed randomly before the cliff, beside the rolling dirt launch ramp. This is it, a launch like a rocket ride, two steps forward, the wings entering into the screaming vertical air flow, bam, body and wings yanked into the sky like a cable hanging from a passing plane just snagged your glider, that damned launch a fucking heart attack every time. I hope my doctor is not reading this, and what about my mom? Would you want your child to act like me, us, Gangreen?

The task is called, the pilots line up single file, the launch window is open, time to party. Wings enter the sky, centering circles over the knife edge black granite spires that slice up through

the green forest canopy, having been forced up from their deep be-
ginnings by inner earth tectonic plate collisions.

Avoiding the Cauldron of Hell, I begin gliding around in the
sky within close proximity to the two thick black cables spanning
the canyons between steel tram towers. So much dynamic action
goes on when flying in a competition thermal: steering the glider,
staying in the lift, avoiding other wings, looking out for cables
while looking through snot-splattered sun glasses. And those
damn cables will not leave me alone. It is as if powerful magnets
are hidden in my harness, or maybe in my subconscious, because I
become, out of no particular reason, attracted to the long steel cables, and whenever I end up flying low on the mountain, bouncing
around the sky in a desperate predicament, these god damned cables keep getting in my face, making me paranoid. Ok, fuck the
cables, I'm out of here. I can take my medicine over at the Cauldron.

There I am yanked up into the sky at dizzying speeds, the
thermals small, like driving a limo around inside a tennis court,
their punch spitting us up at 1,800 feet per minute and then, on the
other side of the thermal, spitting us out and down at 1,800 feet per
minute, the glider acting as if attached to the bottom of the space
shuttle by a bungee cord and we are continually snapping each
other.

Flying a hang glider safely in these conditions is challenging
at best, and survival means flying fast, slicing through the thermals
like a knife through a gun fight. The sky just has its way with you
and you hang on and don't let go. At times like these, life in the
sky is bouncing around severely, egos are put to the test, powerful
G Forces flex their muscles, punishing and thrilling your body together, sweat streaming from your helmet, blowing speckled pat-

terns across your sun glasses, the wise pilot living with the speck-les, not taking his hand off the base tube for nothing, planning on cleaning the lenses once reaching the tranquility of cloud base. Squeezing the base tube with hands securely is like gripping the handle bars of a crotch rocket motorcycle that has a slippery seat; the base tube is your life line to survival. And letting go of it at the wrong time, or relaxing your grip when Mother Nature's powerful, invisible air currents catch you unprepared, your hands will be separated from the tube in the blink of a shooting star and, hands suddenly empty, you grasp into blank space where the base tube used to be, as the wing, without your input, pitches straight up, creating a 50/50 chance of getting flipped over and breaking.

Now picture 90 pilots, each in the company of a bad dance partner, bouncing around the sky like ping pong balls in a lottery drawing, flying tip-to-tip across a three dimensional court, half the flock flying with a new dive recovery system installed on a ques-tionable glider. Then, all of us, at a pre-determined time, race on course, flying directly over a large orange tarp that is rolled open in a field three miles west of the mountain range at exactly high noon, and take a picture of it, proving we were there and entering us into the race. A big glass thermal full of bouncing ping pong balls, racing out over the field just as the tarp fully opens, each pi-lot taking their hands from the base tube and looking through their cameras' view finders, taking pictures of the tarp, while the other pilots that are flying right next to them are taking their hands off the controls to do the same thing. It is like a swarm of drunken bees causing an adrenalin rush to the point if insanity. Totally fucking insane, and I love it. Maybe I was dropped on my head as a child, maybe I was dropped on my head as an adult, maybe I need a shrink, maybe I need a drink, maybe an inoculation, and maybe I just need another joint.

After taking the photos and gliding back to the mountain, the whole flock gaggles together, climbing back up to cloud base where the temperature is tasty cool at 16,000 feet, and the environment is much saner.

Four thousand feet over the peak, with the rest of Gangreen, we commit our corpses to glide over the backside of the range, crossing tree-lined ski runs, leading to parking lots surrounded by power lines, beyond a sea of aspen and then scrub oak, followed by deep cactus-filled arroyos, and enter the dry flat lands on course with plenty of altitude to spare for Taos. From this high perch, the earth appears spotted with sage and pinion trees and Mother Nature's in a much better mood than on the tarp side of the range, presenting us with strong wide thermals and low wind speeds, giving the large flock of bird people room to spread out, and begin the business of racing. Seeing the lead gaggle four miles ahead of us and circling in good thermal, Gangreen puts it into overdrive: eye-watering G-force racing at 50 miles per hour through the sky, entering the elevator ride below the top guns, with 30 more pilots right behind. Some of the more gutsy pilots continue on glide beyond us, across the open sky, hoping to find a faster climbing thermal and getting to goal sooner. We watch as they fly for the horizon. Five miles ahead of us on course, one lone pilot starts to circle, and Dogz says, "Let's go get 'um," and we leave our overcrowded thermal, racing for the new lead gaggle of one.

We continue playing the race-ahead game until we reach the foothills of the Sangre de Christo Mountains, where the cool pinion forests grow and the lift becomes much lighter. But we are racing in overdrive, running wide open, and by the time we notice the lack of lift, possibly due to the greenery not reflecting the heat as well as the hot desert floor, it is too late. We should have been slowing down, shifting into third or even second gear, being patient instead of trying to be heroes, but just get ourselves to goal. Our high-speed mistake catches Gangreen close to the ground and flying in survival mode, struggling in every piece of lift to stay aloft. Way up above us, floating slowly over our heads, the top gun pilots show us why they are top gun pilots. Now Gangreen the team is turning into me, myself and I, as every man for himself works the light thermals near the ground, milking every ounce of power they possess. That is racing: "One minute you're a hero, and the next you're a zero." I lose the lift, finding no more oozing up from the ground below. Time to save me from myself, time to glide efficiently across the sky, getting as close to goal as possible, the closer the more points, and hopefully beat Dogz, saving the team from having to wear the dreaded heat-conducting black clothing that he will have earned the personal right to choose from out of the team's matching wardrobe if he wins the day.

I reach as far as the wing's aerodynamics will let me, setting up for a landing in a nice green sagebrush-covered field. At a distance, it looks like a nice sagebrush-covered field, but when I commit to it, like a double-dealing lover, the field turns out to be a courtyard full of Cholla cactus. You know the cactus with all the arms, covered in two-inch needles that can jump across a three foot ditch?

"Oh shit."

Two choices for landing: the penal colony full of Pongee sticks or the rock hard pinion trees. I choose incorrectly. Flaring the glider between two big cacti, my speed a little fast due to my panicked personality, I pile head first into the jumping haystack full of needles. Coming to a stop, the pain reaches my brain instantaneously. Sharp cactus spines imbedded into my knees and in my shoulder. I am adhered to the plants like a piece of Velcro.

Cholla of pain

Slowly, painfully, hoping to hell the glider is not going to be blown by the wind, dragging me further into the needles, I begin peeling myself away from the plants. If I'd had any drugs or alcohol at the time, I would have ingested them, even knowing that they wouldn't have helped the pain. I set my ass down on a rock, next to my broken glider, the glider looking like a piece of Styrofoam that tangled with a porcupine. I slowly unfold the pliers incorporated into my survival knife, and begin the gasping facial expression pin cushion surgery from hell.

The Mountain King came to a stop on the dirt track next to where I sat on a rock playing tug of war with my tweezers. My teammates piled out of the vehicle and looked at the scowl on my face and sensed the frustration in my heart. Usually the banter amongst my teammates starts with our failure in not making goal but today they showed their softer side, a change in their personalities that surfaces when one of their kind is in pain. They try to make me feel better and offered me some liquor that thankfully I pour over the patches of imbedded spines and down my throat. Then I hobbled into the back of the van sitting still, attempting to avoid driving any outstanding needles deeper into my flesh. Here I sit wondering about my mistakes and how they are shaped. Do they come from my luck or lack thereof – maybe; my stubbornness-a good chance; my ego -a high probability; my fate- yes my fate it is the perfect rational I use for all my short comings. Rationalizing my failures drives my desire; to persevere helps me to recover from just another psychological beating. That night, I spend three hours plucking green and black cactus needles out of my soft white skin. You know the kind, where the skin raises up with imbedded broken- off cactus spine until it is shaped like a volcano and feels like a volcano and pops like volcano and bleeds like a volcano, and all this geology deadened with the help of my anesthesiologist, Dr. Jose Cuervo. I sleep by passing out.

On a painful morning in the warm desert altitude, I feel sunrise. At the pilots meeting on Day Two of the Sandia Classic, the pilots huddle on top of the mountain as the weather man begins his report, explaining that a fast moving cold front, colliding with an Albuquerque low, will be bringing high winds and scattered tornados to the region, all in all an excellent day for pulling cactus quills out of my skin. But that fun activity needs to be held later; just because there are possible tornados and the race is called off, that's no reason for Gangreen not to be going flying. While we put our gliders together, a commotion starts towards the rear of the set-up area and the word spreads through the pilots that a tornado has been spotted touching down 15 miles east, along the peak of South Mountain. Clamoring to the correct location, a flock of 90 very intimidated bird brains looks through the opening in the forest wall to see the dark spinning thermal/tornado worming its way across South Mountain, its energy opening a dreaded darkness in our minds.

Gangreen continues setting up. In a theatrical act of animation, the meet director, freaking out about the tornado, closes the launch window, meaning no one can fly. But this is national forest and only the US Forest Service can dictate their Nazi laws here, and we're Gangreen and we can do whatever stupid thing we want, damn it. We continue, dragging our feet, hard, even though we boast how we want to commit aviation within reach of scattered tornados. Are we nuts?

With the tornado dissipated and the clouds parting, Gangreen and others take to the skies, flying with one eye on our direction of travel and the other scanning the horizon for funneling disaster. Following a short flight with the team over a big grassy field, I begin noticing the landing field spotted with Cholla as I set up my landing approach, their presence delivering a chill up my spine, making my final turn into the field passionate. My landing is, thankfully, a non- event, the short intense flight concluded, but my sensitivity is still with the cacti staring at me in the field, sending out their bad vibes, their cactus arms pointing at me and snickering to each other, pleased about the amount of quills some of their cacti brothers had gotten under my skin. With the rest of my day free, it is time for a hotel room, marijuana, whisky, TV, tweezers and tears as Dogz and I pull the mighty small, yet mighty painful, remnants of my earlier desert disaster.

Day Three of the Sandia Classic starts like any other day on the mountain: violent thermals in front of Sandia, followed by the dreadful start-tarp photos, then climbing to cloud base and running over the back of the range, escaping the mountain, penetrating into the desert, relaxing some and flying free into the wide open. Crows and bugs, straw and insects, hang gliders and plastic bags drift and circle with the wind, crossing the ground together in small flocks following today's task, straight down the asphalt highway 100 miles to Las Vegas, New Mexico.

Observing your surroundings while circling in the sky is like a repetitive slide show, only half of each circle is seen until you circle back around to see what was beyond your wing in the previous circle. When I notice these three dots that look out of place on the northern horizon, I don't think them a threat, and during half the circle I wonder what the hell those are. I have never seen those dots in the sky before. As the circle faces me away from the dots, I curiously wait for them to come back around, and the glider turns until the circle finally comes back around facing north for another look at the unregistered three dots.

Not now, not three small dots, no, three large dots instantly closing the distance in the watering of an eye. My eyes turn the three dots that are way too close into three military green dots, three F4 phantom fighter jets migrating south at our elevation, headed directly at our vertical column of hang gliders, the jets' fuselages bedecked with spikes sticking out from the jets' fronts, ready to skewer an impending column of birdmen shish-kabob style. Their dark green, hard steel wings slice into the gaggle of hang gliders like axes tossed as Frisbees. I scream into my microphone, not a warning, but a scream of instant adrenaline, its violent tone alerting the other pilots. Other helmeted heads turn their fiberglass openings to the direction of the jets. Blood and bone instantly know what I am shrieking about. The hang glider helmets and the fighter jock helmets spot each other simultaneously. It all happens so fast. Flying in a V formation, the three dots are now upon us, giving the military fighter pilots a good two seconds to perform evasive maneuvers. The hang gliders float like balsa wood in line for an impact from a shell shot from a battle ship. Part of Gangreen's standard equipment is a disco ball, nothing technical, just a small Styrofoam ball covered with tiny mirrors that reflect the sunlight, helping fighter pilots to notice us one second quicker. Maybe I have that small disco ball to thank for being alive today. Coming for us three fighter pilots, flying in a V formation like in the war movies, wing tip to wing tip, with the point of the V aimed for the heart of the gaggle. I am unable to move, we're all unable to move, our top speed 80, their launch speed 150. Only reaction speed matters now. Both wingmen traveling on the sides of the V react correctly, sticking one wing up and the other down, banking instantaneously away from the balsawood cutouts, escaping impact by carving away from the column of gliders. The fighter pilot in the middle, however, is pinned in place by his two wingmen, unable to maneuver right or left- lest he hit his fellow fighters. He has nowhere to go. He's fucked and so are we. One stuck in the middle fighter pilot, with years of training so ingrained in his brain, reacts so perfectly, picking an opening between two of us, rotating his wings vertically, he slices between me and another piece of hanging skin and bones with a wing span to spare. Usually I close my eyes just before impact, but this I have to see, even if it's the end of me.

Seeing the writing on the underside of his wing, with an arrow pointed at his fuel tank, makes my body convulse, my hairs stand on end, my adrenaline struck by a baseball bat, the roaring jet's engine noise cruel to my ears, my microphone blown out by my screams. I await the jet wash, thinking, "This is it," but no violent air currents come to break my glider, and by the time I turn and run away, the fighter jets are already a mile gone. My body pulses from the rush and I spend my escape looking behind me, searching for any leftover hang gliding carnage, possibly a parachute canopy tumbling out of the sky.

I can just imagine what was said, back on the nearby military base, by the three fighter pilots in the debriefing room with their commanding officer upon completion of their training mission over the Sandia Mountains.

F 4 Phantom

"Yes, sir, hang gliders."

"No, sir, I do not know where they came from."

"Yes, sir, 16,000 feet. Yes, sir, 400 knots."

"Yes, sir, it was extremely close."

"No, sir, we have no damage to report."

"No, sir, we believe they received no damage."

"Yes, sir, I am sure it scared the shit out of them. Yes, sir, it certainly scared the shit out of us, too."

With my microphone out of commission and my psyche rattled, my glider continues to drag me through the sky until I finally wither away, unable to regain my composure, I landed near the highway in a yellow pasture with a few others pilots who have not made goal, a few other pilots who give me a beer, a few other pilots who shake their heads at the story I tell.

Day Four, I am scared to set up: tornados, cacti, jets…what the hell am I doing? This day turns out to be eventless. Launching into the void, the stress washes off as my concentration returns, the task is called, our day is floating over the wide open brown and dusty desert for a nice long workout of climb and glide and relax and fly, cold fingers up high and sweaty helmet down low, pilots spinning around each other like ice cubes in a swirling tall cool glass. Off in the desert distance, mirages of lakes disappear as we climb higher; thousands of feet below us a straight strip of black asphalt highway splits the burlap of the earth's crust. Attached to the asphalt by gravel roads, truck stops, and small neighborhoods, the massive Sandia Peak disappears into the desert haze beyond the horizon. Millagro is to be today's goal, and Gangreen and 70% of the competitors make it. Millagro is a speck on the map, with one old broken-down building, a gathering place for rats. Maybe at night some old ghosts roam the grounds of the one dilapidated structure, but today it is filled with a happy flock of sunburnt, giddy wing nuts. Ah, a rum and Coke never tasted so good. The exuberant, happy folks reaching goal today act as if they have never grown up, a bunch of children with no adult supervision running free in a world measured in open-ended blocks of time: recess time, story time, dinner time or nappy time. Flying all day was our recess time, happy children landing at goal soon competing for story time, children gesturing skyward, buoyant about their tales of adventure. Then the whole field rolls up and drives back to the hotels, 100 miles away, washing hands and face for our dinner time, and more story time, and then nappy time. *Zzzzzzzzzzzzzzzz!*

Gangreen, flying hard, is actually racking up some competition points and ends up forgoing any practical jokes and just flying like we were born to do. Two more days living in the sky, of high desert flying, drifting downwind in the swirly, bird-filled thermals, one thermal including eight crows, their black beaks cawing at our interruption of their party, incredible height sightseeing, chaffing sunburnt lips, sore muscles, swollen puss-filled skin humps of leftover cactus spines, a couple of flat tires punctured while chasing Dogz into the land of Oz,

His landing location a glowing landscape of surreal orange reflective sunset moonscape. What an excellent time to be a human being.

With the meet over and our goodbyes said, the rest of the team goes home while CG and I head south in the Mountain King in search of more adventure, finding more than we bargained for.

Hobbs, New Mexico is as flat as it gets. No crystal meth here, this is heroin country. Zombies walk the sidewalks with fists surrounding brown paper sacks, and semi-automatic weapons holstered on their hips. Law in this little Wild West town is what you can get away with, and even the county judge carries a 20-round clip. Hobbs, New Mexico. A place where a full-size diesel pickup is butchered into a low rider and no one cares, a place where the bars are surrounded by low-riders and the pickup line in the bar is, "Hey, baby, nice tooth." I took a beating in Hobbs, New Mexico, like a cow released alive from a slaughter house, the rotten meat taste never leaving my mouth, but I hear it is a fine place and I will try it again, someday.

Hang gliding over the flatlands of Hobbs is basically getting yanked into the sky like a kite on a string and letting the wind blow you high across the desert. The goal is to travel as far as possible. There are no tarp starts, no insane multi-tiered gaggles to deal with, it's just you and maybe one or two others competing against Mother Nature, trying to stay in the sky as long as possible and let the wind push, push, push you across the landscape, wandering as far as is achievable before dark.

An old abandoned air force base is located in the middle of the flat desert, empty except for two parallel 10,000 foot long con- crete runways facing directly into the consistent southwesterly wind, as if the Air Force left them behind for our towing pleasure, our tax dollars finally paying off, thanks boys. The B52's gone, the P51 Mustangs gone, their replacement wings traveling over the runways without motors, aircraft needing no fuel, no control tower, and minimal ground crew. Maybe the past heroes of the WW II Air Force are rolling in their graves, watching our gliders dance over their airfield as we use their beloved training grounds any way we please.

Getting a glider and pilot into the sky without an elevated launch is accomplished by towing gliders aloft using custom winches mounted onto the backs of trucks. The tow pilot rests his glider's base tube in small saddles on the tailgate of the truck, where it lies horizontally in its flying position, wing set on the correct angle to the sky and a release line attached to the nose. The pilot climbs onto the truck and is hooked into the glider. He is then personally connected to the end of a rope that is strung across the truck's cab and attached to the winch's spool, the rest of the rope wound onto the spool a length of line 2,000 feet long. The pilot lying prone in his harness in the back of the truck as if flying, dressed for 15,000 feet and sweating in the 90-degree heat, he is now ready to go. He gives the truck driver the nod, "Go to cruise." The truck driver rolls down the runway. The pilot shouts, "Accelerate!" which is short for, "Get my hot ass down the road and into the sky before I melt." The truck driver punches the accelerator, increasing the pilot's excitement as the pilot concentrates on his airspeed display, the wind moving past the wing increasing to ten, twenty, thirty miles per hour, and at thirty five mph, the pilot hits the release button, setting the nose of the big kite free from the truck, air flowing underneath, lifting the wings, flying like a home run hit out of the ballpark. It is so beautiful to watch. Its beauty is that it makes available the miracle of human flight, of soaring like a bird, to citizens of the great American Midwest or anywhere else that mountains tend to get in the way.

Me and CG have never towed up before, and we show up late to the hang gliding meet. Like all good vulture packs, the birds coming late to the carcass are relegated to receive the scraps. Our scrap is a piece of shit tow rig, a contraption made in the garage by some wanna-be-inventor, built with whatever leftover materials he had lying around. We are relegated to this piece of shit tow rig for the meet, the rest of the pilots treat us like bad students demoted to the back of the class. The tow rig looks like an overbuilt sewing machine, and using the thing to haul our gliders aloft makes me afraid.

One at a time, pilots roll down the parallel runways, reel their kite strings away from the trucks and release 2,000 feet above CG, who is still fucking around with the vulture scrap-bloody rib cage-piece of shit tow rig.

Eight more pilots cruise one at a time over our earthbound heads, released from the trucks, liberated from gravity, gaining elevation, as they circle and eventually glide out of sight over the horizon, and still CG fucks with the piece-of-shit tow rig on the ground.

One pilot comes in for a landing and pounds it badly, but he is ok, we all suppose. It looks like he may have injured his glider, but he gives it a quick once-over and deems it airworthy.

Round three, and the pilots begin to tow up without us again. CG is still, well, you know the rest. Out of the sky, above the parallel runway, a hair-raising scream is forced into our ears, a scream not like in the movies, where you sit in a nice cozy seat and get frightened by an actor, oh, no, you have never heard this kind of scream unless you have been in a field of battle. This is a I know I am going to die in ten seconds shocking guttural shriek, like a sick piece of chalk earsplitting across a blackboard of pain. Me and GC turn to look for the source of the involuntary vocalized ending, regretting our instinctive reaction as we watch the last ten seconds of the boy's life. His name was Eric, just like mine but spelled different. From 100 feet up, his helmeted head leading, his glider following, his momentum falling like a steel beam, his life freefalling straight down, plunging as fast as a hang glider will go and knowing his death is imminent, he screams himself into the pavement and finishes his life with a sickening crunch, the impact sounding like a speeding motorcycle hitting a trash truck. We don't know what happened. Maybe when he landed hard earlier, he missed some damage done to his craft or he got hit by a freak atmospheric anomaly or he snagged something on the tow line, but whatever it was he didn't see- it killed him.

On the ground, we are stunned. What the fuck? Is this nightmare in New Mexico really happening and is it ever going to end? I look to CG and he recognizes that I am lying when I say to him, "That pilot is dead and I am not going over there." And CG, acting like my father (and, in a sense, I felt he was), ordering me to go to the tragedy because I am the closest person to the deceased – if only by proximity – and again I say, "I am not going over there," and again CG says, "You got to."

Oh, God, why me?

I run to the heaping pile of death, my head murky, my stomach full of butterflies, my emotions already twisted, I reach the pile of aircraft lying on the runway and belly across the concrete, under the wing, and observe the inert object that once was alive underneath. His eyes are open, radiating a death stare, a stare that I have come to understand, no pulse, no breath, no injuries that I can distinguish, but the helmet looks cracked, and in the shadow of the glider his face gives the impression of being distorted. I roll my finger around inside his mouth and it is clear. I pull his chin down, put my mouth upon his and prepare to perform CPR, but the pressure of my face upon his stretches his skin apart and his nose sinks into the gap where his skull previously joined his face together. His face implodes the tip of his nose level with his eyes. Reluctantly, I gave him a few quick breaths, blood squirting like a fountain from his ears, his red emotional life landing on my arms. He is dead and I am disintegrating. I crawl from under the glider, standing in the way of the approaching paramedics, trying to save

them from the gore. They ask me what the hell I am doing and I
tell them he is dead. Like all good paramedics should, they continue where I left off, but to no avail. I drift to the sandy divider
between the runways, alone questioning my soul. Why am I always chosen to see this carnage? Am I supposed to learn from
these events or is it Karma from my past life coming back to get
me? Have I ever treated anyone so badly in this life that I'm worthy of this pain? Am I just cursed by some unknown entity who is
trying to crush my spirit?

I get down to my hands and knees and wretch and then I cry,
his blood on my arms not letting me go, and I cry some more. He
was so young and it was so avoidable, if only someone would have
told him to wait, or at least looked at his wing or asked if he was
ok, or I don't know what. Hindsight is running roughshod in my
mind, as if a lawnmower spinning over gravel, my self-pity making
me more insane.

It is time to move on. CG brings me some water and what
comfort he is able to provide, which is not much because his emotions are hidden deep, and mine have now erupted to the surface.
Once the mess is carried away, the glider towing continues. CG
and I put our tails between our legs, our desire for flying gone. We
break our gliders down, as our emotions are breaking down, the
result of bad gravity acting up on the parallel runway. We load our
equipment into the ever-reliable Mountain King and roll its tires up
the highway, the King pointed north, running away from the desert, headed for the high country, drinking 86 proof from a paper
bag, me and CG drive back to Colorado in silence.

(Driving home in silence.)

CHAPTER TWELVE

Flying Alone

My wings attached, my equipment prepared, I am standing on launch, looking out over the handsome Colorado mountains. A warm wind is lifting the wings – they are ready to be set free; today I fly alone. Running into the breeze, I enter the sky, cushioned currents support me. Shifting my weight to the right, I bank the glider up on a tip and turn the craft, its momentum sweeping across the face of the hill, below, pine trees and sage brush flow past me in a blur. I lie down in the harness and zip up. Traversing above the earth, I am free. I fly through bobbles of up drafts and down drafts along the far end of the ridge, a thermal rushes up from the ground and I stand the wing on a tip, entering the vertical rush of air, its velocity forcing me up and, equally, gravity resists my body's momentum. This thermal is smooth like chocolate milkshake. Around and around I drive, gaining against gravity. Half way to cloud base, I begin to reflect on my past.

All these years of living on the edge, I feel fortunate to be alive. Hang gliding has been my life, something I was born to do, and though these wings have tried to kill me, if it wasn't for them, who knows where this wild child would have ended up? Far below me, another wing enters the sky. It is JT, tamer of The Wild Thing. We still fly together. From this height, he looks like a white mosquito. I reach the wispy cool moisture of cloud base, stop turning and go on a straight line glide, high above the rolling sage brush terrain, pushed by the wind.

Most of the time when I fly my wing, I leave the mental bonds of earth behind, but today my old friends seem to want to tag along. Thinking back, Gangreen is no more. CG and me, we don't fly together anymore, and I miss him. He lives close by, but an emotional wedge, formed by my ugly fall from Gangreen, is now welded in place and separates our friendship. CG, thanks for sharing. The freedom that was once Gangreen became entangled in a meth binge, and as our personalities unraveled, life as a team became no fun. The team traveling to the competitions, locked in the Mountain King, had begun to resemble a cage match political fight for who controlled who and who is in charge of what. Our once stout friendship slowly split like firewood. The final days, for me, were when the team went to Australia with a we don't give a shit about how you feel attitude, and, like a prisoner on a hunger strike, me and my thin skin left.

Escaping my mind and back into the sky, I pilot the wing across the face of a tall sage-covered hill that is baking in the sun where I hoped a thermal would be waiting for me. Yes, my judgment is correct, finding yet another thermal. Maneuvering to enter it, I spin my wing up like a ballerina on a toe and start to climb. I am hoping to see Dogz as I look out past my wing at the lonely horizon, hoping to see that crazy Injun looking out from his helmet, past his wing, gauging my next move as if we were partners in a ballet. But he is not here.

Dogz is gone. He'd had enough, too, and left Colorado to return to his previous life before we became ballet partners. I never see him and only hear rumors of him filtering through Colorado about his life, but he is always in my heart and, when he reads this book, Dogz, thank you. Thank you for showing me how not to take life so intensely, how to avoid needing to be the alpha male, and how to enjoy each day because each day is a good day to live.

The hiss of my wing and the beep of my Vario disturb a small herd of antelope that have been grazing on the grassy hilltop that I fly above. My shadow sweeps across their backs and the herd mistakes me for a predator as they pick up speed. I feel so much better now that I have quit the drugs, but back in the day I did feel awfully good doing drugs. Isn't that the reason I did them in the first place? It is just that the brain said no more, and age makes recovery so much more obnoxious. Maybe after this flight, I will have a beer, but that is my limit. It's funny, I used to not know my limits. None of us knew our limits. We were like a wolf pack in search of sustenance; curiosity pushed us too far into uncharted territories, and we became lost.

Down below me, the wind lines on the ponds start to increase, the tall grass swirls with the power of the thermals crossing the cattle fields, where the cows are the size of BB's. A single engine airplane passes a couple of thousand feet beneath me and I wonder if he even knows I am here. Off towards the sun, two crows and a red tailed hawk are turning up under a cloud shaped like a mushroom. I glide for them, hoping to continue my journey and make friends.

The crows are cawing to each other and the red tail is high above, marking the thermal's drift as I enter the dance, the crows no doubt thinking I am too weird. They decide to leave me to my climb alone.

I used to need to bond with people, but now I try to bond with crows. I used to fear being alone, but now alone is fulfilling. It seems that alone is where I can let my feelings be felt and my mind to melt. It feels to me that humans are animals, and maybe Gangreen was like the wolf pack, each of us struggling to be the alpha. The shit that goes through my head sometimes surprises even me. Five minutes later, I enter into the wispy white arms of the cloud. It is so peaceful in here, a feeling of déjà vu, maybe I have been in this cloud before. I lose the lift and ooze out the side. Pulling the base tube in for speed, I drive to the crossroads on the highway below. Here I must decide: one road leads over the big mountain range, the other around the corner, through low saddle of the continental divide. I choose the safer side over the divide.

Crossing a small canyon headed south, I notice the two previous crows have caught up with three others of their flock and now five crows are playing together in a thermal being born out of the canyon. I glide past them to my target, an ancient volcanic cone 2,000 feet tall, its rounded top covered in hidden treasures, lava cliffs and a forest blanket.

Fate brought Gangreen together, three people of three diverse backgrounds, following mankind's oldest dream, a dream we pushed to the limits, living a great journey in the process and eventually pushing past the edge of sanity.

I sweep over the top of the volcanic cone, but not a single thermal is breathing here. I fly beyond the trees and pass over a brown sage-covered field, where I see the red tailed hawk ascending out of the dirt. I hook into the lift above him, and what a rough bastard this thermal is, bouncing me around like a gumball in a fish bowl, but I want to continue my flight and I am going to have to take the punishment. I soar to 15,000 feet, having been beat up enough, and calculating I have plenty of altitude to reach the fields on the other side of the mountains, I cross the Continental Divide. Where the highway cuts through the trees on top of the pass, I find another thermal and drift, circling inside it, watching the mountain range unfold beneath me.

What an adventure Gangreen was. Would I change anything that happened during those years? Yes, but only one. Maybe Gary is flying along with me in spirit over this pass. If I knew back then what I know now, I would still not have been World Champion, but because I took people flying under my wing, I feel that is my championship.

Off in the distance, I see the majestic Sangre de Cristo
Mountains. Up wind, JT calls on the radio, "Where are you?"
I tell him my location;" just this side of heaven".

This side of heaven.

Received: April / 30

Dear Gangreen

When Dogz informed me of the adventures of Gangreen I was green with envy. I was instantly depressed at not being able to participate in what must the most exciting team sport since the days of Blackbeard. The thought of you guys jumping off various launches in green was a scary one indeed. However after some careful consideration I have decided to formally apply for a position with you. There can be no greater honor than to wear green and terrorize the skies with such an infamous band of pilots.

I would consider an entry level position with your group. My list of skills includes, good pilot, great attitude, can mix rum and coke, drive, find cheap hotels, find women, locate not greasy restaurants, use the handicap routine on unsuspecting law enforcement officials, whip CG's ass should he need it and , seriously, do anything it takes to contribute to Gangreen. Further, I can stand up to the stringent standards of conduct, dress and attitude which the team adheres to. Just tell me what I got to do to be GREEN!

Regardless of whether you ain't got a spot or you don't think I would behave; I wish you swashbucklers from Color Adoo the best of luck. FLY FAR, FLY FAST, FLY GREEN & RULE THE SKY.

Sincerely
Frank Z.

EK Eagles in the flesh

To experience the freedom of flying go to a Hang Gliding school.

To find a Hang gliding school go to USHPA.com.

"To find your dreams follow your heart".

<u>Disclaimer</u>
This team of pilots pushed beyond any reasonable social norms, though we are but one percent of the great world of Hang Gliding, the other ninety nine percent of pilots in this world, cringe at the behavior of we few.

To order more copies of Eagles in the flesh please go to Eaglesintheflesh.com

Or send a check or money order
for $14.95 plus $3.00 shipping to :
Erik Kaye
Po. box 472
Gunnison, CO. 81230

Erik_kaye@msn.com

Erik Kaye never grew up. In 1976 at the age of 17 with just enough gas money and a well-used VW Beetle he chased his dreams of flying from Illinois to Colorado. In the summer of 1981, under a blue bird sky on the foot hills of the Rocky Mountains he took a Hang Gliding lesson, during which his feet released from earth and he never looked back – until 2010 when he was knocked from the scaffold by a crane and his back was broken. Retiring his wing he was then content to look back, and piloting his fingers across keyboards he wrote about his experiences

Free as a bird @ Crested Butte, Colorado

Eagles in the Flesh, Erik Kaye's memoire of his wild and wooly hang gliding adventures, is highly entertaining. He tells the adventures of the Gangreen Gang, a hairy-chested bunch of Colorado-based hang gliding maniacs who travel the world competing with the world's best. Though rarely finishing in the money, the Gangreen flyers almost always lead the pre-flight, post-flight and sometimes in-flight consumption and abuse of various substances. The resulting tales are usually hilarious and often surprisingly moving in their description of the beauty of flight, the majesty and danger of high altitude weather and the constant search for suitable landing areas in inhospitable terrain. From the Colorado Rockies to the jungles of Brazil, the Gangreen boys party hard and try to lead every takeoff even as they mourn the occasional death of a comrade whose wing collapsed. As a retired pilot with lots of night attack time, Erik's stories took me back to the days when flying was thrilling and we were bullet proof. I always wondered what hang gliding was like; and I'm sure glad I didn't meet Erik until I was too old to try it. One hell of a book.

T.I. Anderson, Colonel (Ret) USAF

As a retired fighter pilot, I truly appreciated the devil-may-care attitude of this highly entertaining book. It was an amazingly wild ride, following Erik through all of his mistakes (and conscious choices) that led to outlandish near-death experience after near-death experience. When I was in high school, I read an uncannily similar autobiographical book by a pioneering, reckless rock climber nicknamed Batso. Within fifty pages of beginning that book I knew I would soon teach myself to climb. I'm probably lucky that I'm now old and wise enough not to follow Erik's lead this time—however I guarantee that there will be many, many people who will. It's really that inspirational. Hang gliding schools, prepare for the onslaught!

E. Tomme, Lieutenant Colonel (Ret) USAF 2000 + Hours, F-4 Wild Weasel. Doctorate Physics, Oxford, MBA.